Achieving QTS
Primary English: Teaching Theory and Practice

Achieving QTS

Primary English:
Teaching Theory and Practice

Second edition

Jane Medwell
David Wray
Hilary Minns
Vivienne Griffiths
Elizabeth Coates

Learning Matters

Acknowledgement
Chapter 8: extract from *The Hodgeheg* by Dick King-Smith (Hamish Hamilton, 1987)
copyright © Dick King-Smith, 1987. Reproduced by permission of Penguin
Books Ltd.

First published in 2001 by Learning Matters Ltd.
Second edition published in 2002.
Reprinted in 2002 and 2003.

British Library Cataloguing in Publication Data
A CIP record for this book is available from the British Library.

ISBN 1 903300 54 1

Cover design by Topics – The Creative Partnership
Text design by Code 5 Design Associates Ltd
Project Management by Deer Park Productions
Typeset by PDQ Typesetting, Newcastle under Lyme
Printed and bound in Great Britain by Bell & Bain Ltd, Glasgow

Learning Matters Ltd
33 Southernhay East
Exeter EXI INX
Tel: 01392 215560
Email: info@learningmatters.co.uk
www.learningmatters.co.uk

CONTENTS

About this book

This book has been written to cater for the needs of trainees on all courses of primary initial teacher training in England and other parts of the UK. By the end of their course, trainees are required to have developed 'skills of planning, monitoring and assessment, and teaching and class management' (TTA, 2002, p. 2). Such teaching skills are required for the award of Qualified Teacher Status (QTS) or its equivalent. The book will also be useful to Newly Qualified Teachers (NQTs) and other professionals working in education who have identified aspects of their English teaching which require attention.

This book has been written with the requirements of the Professional Standards for Qualified Teacher Status firmly at its core. Section 3 of these Standards describes the teaching skills essential for those to be awarded QTS. Specifically, these skills include the ability to plan appropriately for the English work of a specified group of pupils, to monitor, assess and record pupils' progress in the various aspects of English, and to teach effectively the material specified in the National Curriculum and the National Literacy Strategy. This book aims to address the essential skills of English teaching as spelt out in these documents.

Features of each chapter of this book include:

- **clear links with the Professional Standards for Qualified Teacher Status;**
- **clear links with the** *Curriculum Guidance for the Foundation Stage* **(DfEE/QCA, 2000);**
- **links to the English National Curriculum for England (DfEE/QCA 1999);**
- **links to the National Literacy Strategy's (NLS)** *Framework for Teaching* **(DfEE 1998) and the Early Learning Goals (QCA 1999);**
- **English knowledge and understanding;**
- **classroom stories to illustrate important points;**
- **research boxes;**
- **practical activities;**
- **further reading;**
- **a glossary of important terms.**

Each chapter of this book addresses the teaching of particular areas of English, such as reading and writing. The subject knowledge that primary teachers need in order to become effective teachers of English and literacy is addressed in the companion volume, *Primary English: Knowledge and Understanding* (Learning Matters, 2002). However, the authors of the present book have also attempted to make clear the knowledge you will need in order to carry out successful English teaching.

What is primary English?

There is a good deal of consensus about what we want children to achieve in primary English, but it can still be difficult to define primary English as a subject. For the purposes of this book we feel that primary English is about acquiring the skills, knowledge and attitudes to become an empowered reader, writer, speaker and listener.

Teaching primary English involves ensuring children learn the skills and processes of *literacy* and *oracy*, but these are not always defined simply. Literacy can be construed as having the skills necessary for effective reading and writing, but this raises many questions. For instance: what degree of expertise must one achieve to be 'literate'? Are some people more literate than others, and what do we mean by this? Does literacy involve reading certain texts and not others? What about media literacy – the ability to 'read' and be critical about media such as TV and the Internet?

The National Curriculum looks very broadly at literacy, aiming for all children to be able to read and write a full range of texts. They should learn not only to decode and encode written English, but also to be critical about what they read so that they can identify the stance of the author and the intended effects on the reader. The National Curriculum aims for children to read a wide range of texts, including electronic texts. In writing, too, the aims of the National Curriculum are not only for children to be able to write in a technical sense, but also for them to be able to write to express themselves and achieve their purposes for writing.

In oracy it is also important to recognise that children need to be able to listen not only to the literal sense of what is said, but also to listen critically and evaluate the veracity, relevance and intent of what they hear – to become critical listeners. The National Curriculum aims to empower children to become critical speakers, too, so that they are able to speak appropriately and effectively in a whole range of situations, whatever the purpose of their speech.

To use reading, writing, speaking and listening skills, children need a great deal of knowledge. They need to know about the technical aspects of speaking, listening, reading and writing if they are to be able to use them effectively. These 'technical aspects' include a vast range of specialised knowledge, for instance, knowing the sounds of English, knowing about word order in sentences, knowing how to listen for the key points from a text. The most important and complex knowledge children must gain is knowledge about how to orchestrate their skills and understandings about reading, writing, speaking and listening effectively. To do this, children need to know about successful texts – these can be written examples of literature or non-fiction, spoken discussions or reports. If children have clear, effective models they can analyse why these are effective and begin to make their own texts effective. All this knowledge is part of primary English.

In addition to skills and knowledge, primary English also involves attitudes. We aim for children to find reading fiction an enjoyable experience, so that they will be motivated to do more. We aim for children to find non-fiction persuasive, interesting or useful. We aim for children to learn from listening and to speak powerfully. These are only a few of the attitudes towards literacy and oracy that we aim for children to develop. The texts by themselves will not develop useful attitudes in children. It is the way the texts are treated by teachers and children that develops attitudes.

Primary English is about empowering children with a range of skills, knowledge and attitudes for schooling and life. Primary English involves studying and creating spoken and written texts. English texts and language are worth studying for themselves and also as a gateway to every other subject in the curriculum.

The Professional Standards for Qualified Teacher Status

The Professional Standards for Qualified Teacher Status include three areas:

1. Professional Values and Practice – defined as the attitudes and commitment to be expected of anyone qualifying to be a teacher;

2. Knowledge and Understanding – defined as an authoritative knowledge of the subject being taught and an understanding of pupils' progress within that subject;

3. Teaching – defined as the skills needed to plan, manage, monitor and assess pupils' learning.

The Handbook accompanying the statement of Professional Standards clarifies these requirements and gives several examples of them in action, as well as of the kinds of evidence that a trainee teacher could use to demonstrate achievement of the Standards.

In this book we are focusing on the third of the above three areas, the skills needed to plan, manage, monitor and assess learning in English, including literacy.

English in the National Curriculum

English in the National Curriculum is organised on the basis of four Key Stages. Key Stage 1 for 5 to 7 year olds (Years 1 and 2) and Key Stage 2 for 7 to 11 year olds (Years 3 to 6) cover the primary range. The components of each Key Stage include Programmes of Study which set out the English that children should be taught: Attainment Targets which set out the English knowledge, skills and understanding that children should attain, and Level Descriptions which describe the types and range of performance that children working at a particular level should be able to demonstrate within each Attainment Target. English in the National Curriculum is a minimum statutory requirement. Since its introduction in 1989 it has been significantly revised three times. The Programmes of Study for English currently include:

- **En1 Speaking and Listening;**
- **En2 Reading;**
- **En3 Writing.**

English in the National Curriculum also emphasises links with other subjects, and suggestions for the use of ICT. Although English will be the specific focus of English lessons it is also a part of most of the other subjects you will teach in the primary years. This offers valuable opportunities to work across the primary curriculum so that children not only gain extra practice in English skills, but use their literacy or oracy in ways which make it more meaningful or develop flexibility and focus.

The Early Learning Goals

The *Curriculum Guidance for the Foundation Stage*, including the *Early Learning Goals*, describes what most children should achieve by the end of their reception year and offers a structure for planning the Foundation Stage curriculum. These documents identify features of good practice during the Foundation Stage (the Foundation Stage begins when children reach the age of 3) and set out the early learning goals in the context of six areas of learning. One of these areas is that of Communication, Language and Literacy. The early learning goals for language and literacy development mirror exactly the NLS key objectives for reception. The aim is for children to continue their learning seamlessly between the Foundation Stage and Key Stage 1.

National Literacy Strategy – Framework for Teaching

The NLS *Framework for Teaching* is a non-statutory document which is intended to supplement the statutory National Curriculum for English and offer a sort of national 'scheme of work' for English. Although schools do not have to use the NLS *Framework for Teaching*, a great many have chosen to do so. The *Framework* identifies objectives for each year group and encourages recording attainment against these. It also ensures that children addressing these objectives study a very broad range of text types as they go through the primary years. Although the *Framework* deals with literacy and does not specifically mention speaking and listening, a great deal of speaking and listening is implicit in the objectives identified in the *Framework* and certain objectives in the *Framework* strongly suggest active drama work. Publications produced to support the NLS have laid great emphasis on this and exemplified both speaking and listening as part of literacy teaching. The *Framework for Teaching* is designed to be used flexibly both for the planning and the teaching of English, but must always be used with the National Curriculum so that speaking and listening are not overlooked.

Statutory and exemplary documentation

DfEE/QCA (1999) *English: the National Curriculum for England*. London: HMSO.

DfEE (1998) *The National Literacy Strategy: Framework for Teaching English*. London: DfEE.

DfEE/QCA (2000) *Curriculum Guidance for the Foundation Stage*. London: QCA.

TTA (2002) *Qualifying to Teach: Professional Standards for Qualified Teacher Status and Requirements for Initial Teacher Training*. London: TTA/DfES.

Professional Standards for QTS

→ *3.1.1, 3.3.2a, 6*

Section 3 of the Professional Standards for Qualified Teacher Status requires that you can plan, teach, monitor and assess English. This involves your being able to plan effectively for the pupils you teach, based on an understanding of their achievements and needs. It also demands that you understand the range of ways in which pupils learn language and how to create purposeful learning environments in which such learning can best be fostered.

The Handbook accompanying the Standards clarifies these requirements and you will find it helpful to read through the appropriate section of this Handbook for further support.

The National Literacy Strategy

The National Literacy Strategy is a text-centred programme with focused objectives at text, sentence and word level which develop language use, language study and learning through language. This chapter looks at some of the principles underpinning this approach to language teaching.

Introduction

This chapter will consider general trends in the way children learn language and draw parallels between literacy and oracy learning. The chapter looks at how you as a teacher can best support children's development as language learners and teach children the range of skills, knowledge and attitudes they need to become effective readers, writers, speakers and listeners. Later chapters focus on how these general strategies are used for different aspects of literacy and oracy teaching at the different age phases within the primary school.

What is language?

Most of us learned our first language so early in our lives that we do not remember doing so and therefore we are able to take this immense learning achievement for granted. When we look at teaching language to others, however, we need to review and establish what it is important to know and be able to do in language. Kavanagh and Mattingley (1972) refer to 'the glass effect' – language, like glass, is totally transparent in use but, like glass, is still there as an object of study. It is important that children use language effectively, automatically and without having to give undue attention to it, but it is also important that they, and you as their teacher, are able to take a close look at language and examine ways of using it more effectively.

Practical task

1. ***List six things you have read and four conversations you have taken part in during the past 24 hours.***
2. ***You are in an airport in Greece but you do not speak, read or write Greek. You need to find your way to the car hire area.***

   Why are you 'lost'?

   What can you do?

   What <u>do</u> you know about Greek?
3. ***Read this passage:***

   Impairments in ______ are overtly manifested in children who exhibit errors in their speech production that are ______ for their age. Phonology is an aspect of linguistic ______ concerned with both the rules governing the ordering of ______ into meaningful units and the ______ phonetic qualities in which meanings are transmitted (Grunwell, 1990). Language ______ include phonological impairments that occur either in isolation or with other ______ problems (Bishop and Edmundson, 1987; Leonard, 1982).

   The relationship between ______ skills and reading has received a great deal of attention in light of the body of research that has indicated that deficits in phonology can be directly linked to ______ disabilities (see Catts, 1989). During the ______ phase, the first stage of formal reading instruction, there is a heavy ______ on a phonological processing method to access ______. Words are broken into graphemes, graphemes are converted into phonemes, and phonemes are blended into ______ to form words. To perform this process successfully, adequate ______ awareness (phonics) skills are required (Blachman, 1989; Catts, 1989; Snyder and Downey, 1991). Children with reading ______ have been found to be poor in tasks that tap ______ awareness: these include sound counting, sound deletion (say 'dog' without the 'd'), sound ______ (reversal of phonemes), and sound ______ (e.g. categorising words by their beginning sounds) (Blachman, 1989).

   Can you get the full meaning from this passage? If not, why is this?
   What strategies do you use to work out the meaning?

Language is functional and meaning orientated

If you look at your list of readings you will find that all the reading you did was meaningful and had some purpose – to provide enjoyment or amusement, to inform you, to persuade you. When you try to read a sign you have an expectation of meaning and function (or purpose) of the sign. In the third task above, you may have been able to supply missing words on the basis of the meaning – your existing knowledge of the subject or ability to work out a plausible meaning. This, in reading, is called using *semantic cues* or information. When you look at the National Literacy Strategy you will notice that great emphasis is placed on children understanding how texts achieve their purpose. This is because by recognising the purpose of a text children can make appropriate language choices.

RESEARCH SUMMARY

The work of Halliday (1978, 1985) and his theory of 'Functional Systemic Linguistics' has been very important in recent years in informing practice in literacy teaching. Halliday's emphasis has been on looking at what language lets us do in the world – its function. Halliday's work has introduced a range of important insights, many of which have been a strong influence on the creation of the National Literacy Strategy (and are equally appropriate to oracy).

- *It has emphasised that language is not just a means of communicating. It is also a way of making meanings and understanding the world. Language is a way of achieving what we want in our culture.*
- *Halliday has looked at the ways language is related to problem solving, thinking, and understanding. He emphasises that ways of using language are at the heart of understanding the ideas and concepts of any knowledge area – this has real implications for how we use language in teaching. For instance, if we want children to think and learn problem solving like mathematicians, they need to learn and use the language and ideas internalised by mathematicians. You, in learning to become a teacher, will learn the language of teaching. This is not just jargon, it is a crucial tool in enabling you to think and problem solve as a teacher and learn the concepts and ideas shared by other teachers.*
- *Halliday has given the world the concept of 'texts' – meaningful chunks of written or spoken language. He argues strongly that the level at which we operate in the real world is not the word or the sentence but the level of the whole text. We, as teachers, need to respond to texts in terms of their success or failure at achieving their purpose for a given audience. It is not coincidence that the National Literacy Strategy is a text centred programme – it aims to teach children to make, use and respond effectively to a whole range of texts. The National Curriculum emphasises this for speaking and listening as well.*
- *Halliday has emphasised 'genres' – forms of language – which are valued in different contexts. This has led to the study of appropriate genres for children to be taught. One effect of this has been that the National Literacy Strategy has not only identified a wide range of important genres (or text types) to teach in literacy, it has also identified the features and effects of those texts so that children can learn how texts function.*
- *Halliday has developed awareness of the relationship between author, purpose and linguistic choice. By making the linguistic choices involved in constructing a written text, or by uttering a spoken text, we are using our knowledge of the purpose of the text and the range of language elements available to us. As teachers we want to teach children to be aware of how language choices change as the audience and purpose of a text change. So, children writing a newspaper report for other children will make different language choices from those writing a letter to the local council. Halliday's work has given many authors a framework for considering how texts work and how children might best learn to create and respond to texts.*

Language is a code

Language might be described as the set of symbols we use to represent our immediate lives as well as experiences and ideas far away from us. Language even lets us represent abstract concepts (such as language or thought). It is certainly a very flexible and creative code. The basic units which carry meaning in English are phonemes and graphemes. At the *word* and *sub-word level* around 45 basic sound units (phonemes) and the 26 letters of the English language, along with spaces, pauses, punctuation marks and intonation, can be combined in a multitude of ways. You cannot read

Greek signs because you do not know the basic units of Greek code. In reading we call using the links between known symbols and sounds using *graphophonic cues*. In the second task above you did not know these basic facts about the Greek language and so you could not extract the full meaning from the Greek signs, but there are probably many things you could understand about a Greek sign. As an English user you knew the function of signs and expected them to contain useful information. You had a concept of word and letter, and even though you could not read the words, you knew in which direction the text proceeded. In a more sophisticated way you knew that there were likely to be sentences and that the word order would be significant. These insights were not enough to allow you to understand the Greek text fully, but they do remind you that all these ideas are important for young children who will understand some, but not all, aspects of the sophisticated code of language.

There are also *sentence level* codes that help us to understand language. In the third task above you probably guessed some of the missing words because you knew so much about the sentence structure around those words that you could predict from the syntax. The code of language at sentence level is called grammar and it is a very powerful way of making meaning. Although spoken language is actually clause driven, rather than reliant on the full sentences of writing, this also has a clear grammar and syntax. We call using known syntactic structures in reading using *syntactic cues*.

At a whole *text level* the codes of language include the ways written or spoken text types are structured for their purposes. As an experienced language user you would know the purpose of a sign or of the texts you have written.

For more on phonemes and graphemes, see Chapter 3 of Primary English: Knowledge and Understanding from Learning Matters.

Children learning language

Interesting insights into how children acquire their early knowledge about the workings of literacy can be gained from considering some of the processes through which they learn spoken language. While learning to talk is not the same as learning to be literate, both processes clearly have much in common, because spoken language has much in common with written language. (Written language also differs in important ways from spoken language, and awareness of these differences is in itself an important feature of becoming literate.) Some of the processes by which children learn spoken language apply to the acquisition of literacy.

Ordinary children, from the moment they are born, are surrounded by spoken language. One of most noticeable facts about babies is that people talk to them long before anyone could expect these babies to understand what was being said. And the remarkable thing about the way people talk to babies is that they generally do it meaningfully. Of course, there is a certain amount of 'goo-gooing', but, more often, the talk will be similar to, 'Who's going to see his Grandad? Yes, he is. Oh, there's a clever boy.' Many babies spend almost the whole of their waking lives being played with; play which almost inevitably is accompanied by talk. This talk may not be in totally adult forms but is invariably meaningful. In addition to this, young children are also surrounded by talk that is not directly addressed to them. Again such talk is invariably meaningful and much of its sense is obvious from its context. Children then begin life bathed in meaningful talk.

Because the talk that surrounds them is meaningful, young children are receiving continual demonstrations of the purposes of spoken language. If an adult says to a child, 'Who's dropped his ball then. There we are. Back again', and returns the ball, the adult is demonstrating the connection between talk and the action it refers to. When the child says, 'Daddy blow', and the adult responds with, 'Yes, Daddy will blow the whistle now', the demonstration is not only of the connection between language and action, but also of an appropriate form of speech. Children receive millions of demonstrations of meaningful talk, not only directed at them, but also taking place around them. From these demonstrations they have to work out how the system of language works so that they can begin to take part in it.

Of course, the simple fact of witnessing demonstrations of language would not be sufficient to turn children into language users unless some other factors were also present. First among these is engagement, that is the desire on the part of children to take part in the language behaviour they see around them. This desire arises because children witness the power of language in the world, and want to share in it. They see, for example, that if you can ask for a biscuit rather than just scream loudly you are more likely to get what you want. They also see that using language in ways that achieve the effects they want is not something so difficult they are unlikely to master it. On the contrary, language is presented to them from the very first as something they *can* do. This produces a crucial expectation of success, which we know to be vitally important in actual achievement. There is plenty of evidence that children, both in and out of school, achieve very much what they are expected to achieve by other people. It is likely that this works because children internalise others' expectations about them, and come to hold these expectations of themselves. The most familiar example of this concerns children whom adults label as 'not very clever', and who come to believe this of themselves. Because they do not believe they can 'be clever', they stop trying to be.

In the case of spoken language, however, every child is expected to be able to master it (unless some medical condition makes this impossible). Asking any parent the question 'Do you expect your child to learn to talk?' is likely to produce only a very puzzled response. The question seems ludicrous because the answer is so obvious. Because the adults around them believe so firmly that they will become talkers, the children themselves come to believe they will do it, and they do, generally effortlessly.

When children are learning to talk, it is highly unlikely that the adult expert talkers that surround them will decide to administer a structured programme of speech training. Adults who have tried to be even a little systematic in helping children to develop language have found that it simply does not work. The following much quoted exchange between child and care-giver is an example of what can happen.

> CHILD: *Nobody don't like me.*
> MOTHER: *No, say 'Nobody likes me'.*
> CHILD: *Nobody don't like me. [Eight repetitions of this dialogue]*
> MOTHER: *No, now listen carefully: say 'Nobody likes me'.*
> CHILD: *Oh! Nobody don't likes me.*

(This exchange comes from the work of David McNeill. It is quoted in Crystal (1987), p. 234.)

Instead of this situation, in which the adult has tried to take responsibility for what the child should learn, it is much more usual for the child to take the responsibility. Learning to talk is the child's task, which can be supported by adults but is not sequenced, structured or taught by them. The majority of adults implicitly accept this and rarely try to force the pace when children are learning to talk, but instead take their lead from the child's performance.

During this learning, nobody expects children to perform perfectly from the very beginning. If children had to wait until they had perfect control of all facets of spoken language before speaking, they would not produce any speech until at least nine or ten years of age. What in fact happens is that children produce spoken language forms which are approximations to adult forms, and these approximations gradually become closer and closer to the desired end-product. 'Baby talk' is not only accepted by care-givers but is actually encouraged by being received with amusement and pride. It is also usually responded to as a meaningful utterance, and elaborated by the adult into a more fully developed form. When a child says, for example, 'Daddy you naughty', the adult is much more likely to respond with something like, 'Oh, fancy saying Daddy is naughty. He's a good Daddy', rather than, 'No. Say 'Daddy, you are naughty'. The adult responds to the child's attempts at fully-fledged speech forms by interpreting and adding meaning rather than by correcting them. Approximations are accepted and responded to by adults, and gradually children realise for themselves that they are approximate and how to make them more 'adult'.

Any learning, to be effective, requires a great deal of practice on the part of the learner, and learning to talk is no exception. For the vast majority of children this is no problem at all. They are constantly surrounded by talk and are expected and given chances to join in with it. Even when by themselves they carry on practising, from early babbling in which language sounds are practised to later oral accompaniments to actions such as play. Significantly this practice occurs for completely different purposes than to help children learn to talk. Adults rarely hold conversations with babies and young children because they know this is good for their language development. Nor do children talk to themselves when playing because they think this will make them better talkers. Both activities occur for more fundamental, human reasons. Conversations take place because there is something to converse about and children are included in the conversation that accompanies everyday action from very early in their lives. Children talk to themselves because this is how they represent their actions to themselves and how they reflect upon these actions. This kind of talk becomes more and more elliptical and eventually fades altogether, occurring inside the head as 'inner speech'. It is the beginning of thought.

For all the importance of the above processes in children's growing capacity to produce meaningful speech, none of them would work were it not for the fact they all operate in a two-sided situation. Children are immersed in language, receive a myriad of demonstrations of it, are expected to try to emulate these and are given freedom and opportunities to do it at their own pace and level of approximation, but the crucial factor is that all this happens in the context of real dialogue with other people. Adults talk, not just across children, but also to them; they expect children to talk back to them, and when they do, adults respond. This constant interaction is at the heart of growing language use. And it is the need for interaction that comes first. Relationships need to be developed and things need to be achieved together. Language comes into being as a means of helping these things happen. It is therefore learned as a means of coping with the demands of being human.

Because of the interactive nature of language learning the process inevitably involves response. Children respond to adult language, and adults respond to children's attempts at language. Such response not only reaffirms the relationship which forms the context of the talk, but also gives children feedback about their language and, perhaps, a more elaborated model upon which to base future language.

The development of insights into literacy

The same processes that underpin the development of spoken language can also be seen to underpin the development of children's early insights into and use of literacy.

The vast majority of children are surrounded by literacy from their earliest years. Here are just a few of the manifestations of this:

- **they consume things covered in print, from soft drink cans to chocolate bars;**
- **they wear print, from clothes labels to T-shirt slogans;**
- **they accompany their parents shopping in printed surroundings and come into contact with signs, from Car Park to Play Centre, and printed packages, from Corn Flakes to Snickers;**
- **they watch print on screen: on television and as part of computer packages;**
- **they see print used in their homes, from shopping lists to telephone directories, and recipes to newspapers.**

This environmental print is not there simply by accident, but because it communicates messages. Children are thus surrounded by meaningful print. They are also continually being given demonstrations of people using this print. They see adults:

- **following instructions on packages and making their food;**
- **reading newspapers, magazines or books, and reacting with laughter, anger, sadness, etc.;**
- **consulting telephone directories, and dialling numbers guided by print;**
- **reading computer screens and bank machines;**
- **finding their way around supermarkets by following the signs;**
- **and so on, ad infinitum.**

These are illustrations that print can affect the way you feel, can act as a guide to action, or can be used for the sheer pleasure of using it. As a result of these constant demonstrations of literacy, most children come to value engagement in literacy. This shows itself in all kinds of ways. Some children learn that there is little point in saying 'I want a burger' unless you are near a place which sells them, which you know because of the signs outside. (American researchers have suggested that virtually every American two- to three-year-old can 'read' the McDonald's sign!) Others will proudly produce a page covered in scribble and say 'I've written a story'. The three-year-old girl who sat for three quarters of an hour absorbed in the pages of a book which was on her knee, upside down, had learnt to value the literacy behaviour she had witnessed in adults, even if she had not quite yet worked out how to do it. Any reception teacher will testify to the fact that most of their new charges come to school wanting to learn to read above all things. Their engagement with literacy is usually high.

Before they reach school, most children have few grounds not to believe that they will be successful in their encounters with literacy. The majority of three-year-olds will cheerfully 'read' a book, even if what they say does not match to the actual printed words. They will also 'write', using scribble or the letters of their name to signify meaning. Because they have received so many demonstrations of literacy in so many contexts, they come to believe that there is nothing to it. Everyone else can do it, so they can too, or even if they are aware they have not quite got the hang of it yet, it is only a matter of time until they do. It is a sad fact that the first time many children begin to doubt that they will master the activities of reading and writing is when their school experience shows them that these things are difficult and failure is possible.

In the early lessons that children learn about literacy it is unlikely that adults will make too many demands upon them to perform in particular ways. The choice of whether to attend to the literacy demonstrations around them and whether to try to copy them or not is left to the children. They therefore, as with spoken language, have responsibility for their own learning. Of course, parents often do attempt more direct teaching of reading and writing with young children than they do of speaking. This is only natural, given the high status of literacy and parents' perceptions that the ability to read and write is linked with success in later life. Most parents will, however, take the lead from their children in terms of how long their teaching will last, when they have done enough and, indeed, what this teaching will consist of. Again the child has a large amount of responsibility for the process.

Adults also rarely expect the 'reading' and 'writing' of their young children to be perfect. A two-year-old who makes up a spoken story in response to looking at a captioned picture book is more likely to receive praise for this effort than an exhortation to be more careful and get the words right. Similarly children who present their parents with scribbled 'letters' are likely to have their attempts taken seriously, with the parents pretending to 'read' the message, and not to be admonished for their poor handwriting or spelling. In the same way that children are allowed 'baby-talk' which approximates to adult speech, they are allowed 'baby-reading' and 'baby-writing'.

In addition to being surrounded by demonstrations of literacy, many children get a great many opportunities to take part in it, at however rudimentary a level. Almost all children 'write', whether it be with pencil, felt tip, crayon, paint brush or chalk. Most of them also 'read', whether from books, comics, TV screens or advertisements. The three-year-old who proudly displays a new T-shirt with Pokémon on the front is using the ability to derive meaning from printed symbols. The two-year-old who picks up the tube of Fruit Gums rather than the indigestion tablets is making discriminations on the basis of print. Reading and writing, in rudimentary forms, are part of most young children's play activities simply because they are such a significant part of their worlds.

Finally, many of children's early interactions with print take place in collaboration with an experienced adult. This is done so naturally that many adults are almost unaware of it. Some examples will show it in action.

- **A mother is shopping with her two-year-old boy who sits in a seat in the shopping trolley. He reaches out and picks up a packet of Corn Flakes. He says, 'Bix, Mummy'. The mother replies, 'No. We don't want Corn Flakes. We want Weetabix. See. Here we are.' She has given feedback on his interpretation of print, and helped him learn more about this process.**
- **A father is standing at a bus stop with his three-year-old son. A bus draws up and the little boy moves forward. The father says, 'No. We want the bus for Warwick Street. This goes to Haslam Road, look.' He points to the indicator on the bus. He is demonstrating which items of print it is important to attend to.**

- **A mother is playing 'Shops' with her three-year-old daughter. She asks to 'buy' several things, and helps her daughter find each item in the shop. Each time the child finds the right item, the mother praises her with, 'Yes. That's the toothpaste'. Again the child is being helped to make links between objects and their print representations.**

Of course, children vary in the quantity of interactions of this kind which they experience with their parents. Where they receive a great many, the children are in fact being treated as apprentice print users, an experience which almost certainly helps them develop into independent print users later. The concept of apprenticeship is an important one in trying to understand the growth of early literacy, and essentially involves the actions of an expert being copied and experimented with by a less expert apprentice. Learning takes place naturally and almost undetectably, yet it clearly does take place.

The experience of literacy that children get at home is probably not sufficient to ensure they develop into fully competent experts in all the ways literacy is used in the modern world. While it is true that most children make a start on the process of becoming literate before they arrive at school, there is a great deal that they still have to learn. However, they have made an important start before they ever enter school. Although school has a vital role to play in the development of literacy, it can still learn a great deal from an examination of the learning processes at work in the home that we have just discussed. The attractiveness of these processes is in their naturalness. The fact that nobody, parents or children, consciously plans these processes suggests that there is something in them that is fundamental to effective human learning. If this is so, these processes represent a very good place to start in planning the teaching that happens in school. As children learn in school, they do become more independent and more able to deal with abstracts, so they can extend their range of learning strategies, but it makes sense to build upon the insights they bring with them from pre-school experience.

Halliday emphasised three aspects of language learning: learning language, learning through language and learning about language. Very young children are engaged in doing all these right from the beginning. As their vocabularies expand (learning language) they learn about using language for the social purposes in their environment (learning about language) and in doing so they learn about the world and their place in it (learning through language). We build on this learning when they come to nursery and school. To do this we need to teach all three of Halliday's aspects of language.

- **Teachers need to offer children more language to learn – more, varied text types (spoken and written), a wider range of words, new ways of organising language, the conventions of standard written English at text, sentence and word levels.**
- **Teachers need to help children to learn about language – to reflect on and analyse how texts work and to speak and write new texts. By learning about language children will become more flexible users of language.**
- **Teachers need to help children learn through language. Children need to learn the language of the subjects they study so that they can learn the concepts of those subjects. Children also need effective oracy and literacy skills so that they can have access to other subjects.**

Practical task

The table below, adapted from that given in David Crystal's Encyclopaedia of the English Language *(1995, p.291) summarises some of the differences between spoken and written language.*

Differences between speech and writing	
Speech is time-bound, transient and part of an interaction in which both speaker and listener are usually present.	*Writing is space-bound, permanent and the result of a situation in which the writer is usually distant from the reader.*
The spontaneity of most speech makes it difficult to plan in advance. The pressure to think while talking produces looser construction, repetition and rephrasing. Long utterances are divided into manageable chunks, but sentence boundaries are often unclear.	*Writing allows repeated reading and analysis, and promotes the use of careful organisation. Units of discourse (sentences, paragraphs) are usually easy to identify through punctuation and layout.*
Because participants are typically in face-to-face interaction, they can rely on such cues as facial expression and gesture to aid meaning. Speech tends to rely on words that refer directly to the situation, such as 'that one', 'in here', 'right now'.	*Lack of visual contact means that participants cannot rely on context to make their meanings clear. Most writing therefore avoids the use of expressions which pin it to the here and now.*
Many words and constructions are characteristic of speech, such as long, conjoined sentences, vocabulary which may have no standard spelling (whatchamacallit), slang and grammatical informality (isn't, he's).	*Some words and constructions are characteristic of writing, such as multiple use of subordination in the same sentence, and the use of precise vocabulary.*
Speech is very suited to social functions, such as passing the time of day, or any situation where casual and unplanned discourse is desirable.	*Writing is very suited to the recording of facts and the communication of ideas, and to tasks of memory and learning.*
There is an opportunity to rethink an utterance while it is in progress. However, errors, once spoken, cannot be withdrawn.	*Errors and other perceived inadequacies in writing can be eliminated in later drafts without the reader ever knowing they were there.*
Unique features of speech include intonation, contrasts of loudness, tempo, rhythm, and other tones of voice.	*Unique features of writing include pages, lines, capitalisation, spatial organisation, and several aspects of punctuation.*

How does having learnt spoken English help the literacy learner?

How is learning written English different from spoken English?

Cambourne (1988) systematically observed toddlers in experimenter-free settings and recorded their talk with care-givers, friends, neighbours and in a range of different settings. He identified certain conditions in the language learning environment which he considered 'necessary' conditions for language learning to occur. Cambourne suggests that these conditions are essential for early literacy learning in classrooms. These eight conditions are summarised below:

- *Immersion. Language learning involves being immersed in language. Babies are immersed in language (and involved in it) from birth. In classrooms children can be immersed in literacy and oracy.*

- *Demonstration. To learn language children need demonstrations of why they use language, how they use language and what language to use. Demonstrations of talking, listening, reading and writing are essential in literacy teaching to show children at all levels what they can do, why they should do it and how to go about it.*

- *Engagement. Immersion and demonstration are not sufficient conditions for language learning. The child must be engaged and take part, or else learning will not occur.*

- *Expectations. Parents give very clear signs that they expect their babies to learn to talk. Teachers need to have clear, high expectations in literacy and oracy learning.*

- *Responsibility. Babies learning to talk initiate much of the talk and take responsibility. So children need to participate in decision-making in school language learning.*

- *Employment. Young children use language long before they have a perfect mastery of it and 'practise' in situations like babbling and pre-sleep monologues. So young literacy learners need plenty of chances to use language for a purpose and to practise.*

- *Approximations. Parents accept approximations from young children and see in them signs of development. Teachers, too, must accept approximations as part of learning literacy.*

- *Response. Parents respond positively and give meaning-based, but usually correct, responses to children's approximations. Feedback is very important in early literacy and oracy work.*

Learning English:

a summary of key points

- *Language is functional and oriented towards meaning.*
- *Language is encoded meaning and successful use of it demands the ability to decode.*
- *The codes of language occur at three levels: word, sentence and text.*
- *There are a number of processes that characterise children's learning of spoken language, such as immersion in meaningful talk and the use of approximations.*
- *Early, pre-school experience of literacy relies on similar processes.*

Further reading

Cambourne, B. (1988) *The Whole Story*. Leamington Spa: Scholastic.

Halliday, M. A. K. (1978) *Language as a Social Semiotic: The Social Interpretation of Language and Meaning*. London: Edward Arnold.

Halliday, M. A. K. (1985) *An Introduction to Functional Grammar*. London: Edward Arnold.

3 EFFECTIVE ENGLISH TEACHING

Professional Standards for QTS

→ 3.1.2, 3.3.3

Section 3 of the Professional Standards for Qualified Teacher Status requires that you can plan, teach, monitor and assess English. This involves your being able to set challenging learning objectives for all your pupils and to use the most effective teaching means for achieving these objectives, in particular organising and managing your teaching time effectively.

The Handbook accompanying the Standards clarifies these requirements and you will find it helpful to read through the appropriate section of this Handbook for further support.

The National Literacy Strategy

The National Literacy Strategy is a text-centred programme with focused objectives at text, sentence and word level which develop language use, language study and learning through language. This chapter looks at some of the key teaching strategies implicit in this.

Introduction

In the previous chapter we considered the key features of language and some of the conditions which support language learning. From these it is possible to draw out some important strategies for teaching English in the primary school. We suggest that the following teaching strategies are features of successful literacy and oracy teaching at all key stages but these teaching strategies will, of course, operate rather differently at the Foundation Stage, and each of the first two Key Stages. We will provide some examples of how this works.

Offer frequent demonstrations

In teaching literacy and oracy the teacher has to offer *demonstrations*, or models, of all aspects of what is being taught because the processes are largely invisible and it would be hard for children to infer them without a model. In reading it is important to demonstrate what reading involves. This means reading enlarged texts so that the children can see the text and read it with the teacher. Big books are popular at Foundation and Key Stage I for this reason. At Key Stage 2, posters and overhead projectors allow teachers and children to share texts. In demonstrations of reading children need to see all aspects of reading:

- **the content – the meaning of the passage and how it is encoded, including the direction of text, concept of word, structures of particular text types;**

- the skills of reading – how the experienced reader works out words or meanings and the strategies used;
- the reader's response to reading – teachers need to demonstrate how the purpose of the text affects the reader. If it is a story, what is enjoyable, and why? If it is a persuasive text, what persuades, and how?

The same is true of demonstrations of writing. Teachers can model writing right from the beginning of nursery provision. This involves demonstrating:

- appropriate content – what goes into each type of writing and how to generate and order ideas;
- the skills of writing – in the early stages this will involve demonstrating handwriting and spacing, spelling and layout. Later, children need to see idea generation, revision and reordering of ideas, editing and changing of texts;
- knowledge of the features of the text type – knowing what the text aims to achieve and how to choose structures, words and ideas to suit the reader.

In speaking and listening teachers also have an important role to play in demonstrating the use of *standard English*, especially as many children may not actually speak standard English but will have a home *dialect* or language of their own. Teachers initially model standard English through their speech with children, but later in school will also model its use by discussing when standard English is, and is not, a good language choice. Role-play and *hot seating* are strategies that involve modelling the use of English. As well as modelling a particular variant of English, the teacher will also model how to achieve particular speech purposes – a report, a discussion or a story-telling. Speech, especially intonation, is a very important aid to making sense and using grammar for reading for early readers.

Demonstrations, or models, are very important in literacy and oracy in showing children what to do and how to do it but they are only useful if children are able to make the links between demonstrations and their own work. Talk is one way to help them do this.

Talk about language

It is important to be able to talk about language choices with children in group, whole-class and individual situations. Talking about language choices and their effects helps children to become better at using language for a purpose. It is important to have a shared vocabulary about language (a *meta-language*) so that issues can be dealt with clearly. Naturally, talk about language becomes more abstract the more experienced the children are, but it would be a mistake to think that only older children can discuss language. The youngest children use terms such as 'story', 'dictionary', 'word', 'letter', 'sound' or 'phoneme' (depending on your preference) and older children can use a very wide range of terms clearly. The National Literacy Strategy Framework of Teaching Objectives includes a glossary of terms that you will find useful. It is also apparent that many teachers of literacy, at all levels, use a great many technical terms with their pupils.

David Wray and Jane Medwell, in their Effective Teachers of Literacy study, found evidence of the following terms being used by literacy teachers:

- **Word level**: *alphabet, alphabetical order, rhyme, definition, beginning sound, middle sound, end sound, vowel, word, letter, sound, blend, magic e, homophone, synonym, digraph, prefix, spelling string.*
- **Sentence level**: *capital letter, full stop, sentence, speech mark, inverted comma, noun, thing word, adjective, describing word, contraction, apostrophe, word order, dialogue, conversation, apostrophe, question mark.*
- **Text level**: *predict, picture, caption, label, paragraph, planning, drafting, revising (plan, draft, revision), story, instructions, report, headings, ending, opening, character, setting, alliteration, ingredients, list, fiction, non-fiction, layout, address, salutation, skimming, scanning, highlight, key word, meaning, expression, image, simile.*
- **Range of text types**: *poem, author, illustrator, paperback and hardback, nursery rhyme, cover, ISBN, picture, script, play, recipe, dictionary, appreciate, comparison.*

It is important, when discussing language, to make sure you are actually discussing how a language element works in the context of a passage, often a shared or guided reading or writing passage or a piece of the child's own work. Simply offering children definitions of language units does little to further their understanding.

Make learning goals clear

It is important to be quite clear about what you want children to learn and why. For you, as a teacher, this is vital to planning effective lessons. For the children as learners it helps them to understand what they learn and to make links between their understandings. For very young children objectives will be simpler than for older children but it still essential to make them clear.

In English lessons for children at Key Stage 1 and 2, many teachers write the objectives of a lesson in a way that is clearly visible for the children. This is useful, as long as you check that children have read and understood these objectives, that they are checking their learning against them and that they are considering when they might use this piece of learning again. Successful English teachers sometimes check these things in whole-class introductions and plenaries.

Have high expectations and targets

Although literacy and oracy learning is not biologically natural, it is a very normal activity in our society and so it is quite appropriate to signal to children that you expect them to learn these processes. Indicating to children that they are likely to find an activity or skill impossible or very difficult can inhibit their progress. As children progress through schooling it is important to set targets for groups and individuals so that they can focus on improving particular aspects of the very complex processes of literacy and oracy. The key to doing this is to assess children's progress diagnostically.

Use language purposefully

Whenever possible, children should understand the purpose of the text they are reading and creating. This gives them a clear view of the reader or author and enables them to make appropriate language choices and responses. It is also good practice for children to see examples of the text type they are working on, examine how that text works and then create that type of text. This is a useful cycle because it gives children a clear context for language study. When you are studying a word or sentence level element of language it is important for children to understand how they will use this element and what its contribution is to the whole text.

Play with language

Play is a vital learning process for young children and it is, in itself, a purposeful activity for them. When young children play with language they are able to explore its purposes, forms and the reactions of others to their use of language. The Curriculum Guidance for the Foundation Stage recommends play as a language learning opportunity. Language play is an important part of the Foundation and Key Stage I classroom.

Classroom story

Mrs S has set up a dramatic play area in her Reception/Y1 class. She changes the theme regularly so that children have three different play settings each term. In the final part of the winter term, just before Christmas, the class have been studying 'people who help us' and have had visits from people in the community, including a postman. Mrs S has made the dramatic play area into a post office for the children to use. To do this she has introduced a suitable table to be a counter and placed on it a till and play money, a post-person's hat, some scales, envelopes and paper and 'pretend' stamps. She has collected a variety of forms for purposes such as TV licences and passport applications from the real post office and made them available in the class post office. The teaching assistant in the school has made a set of parcels of various shapes and sizes, containing a range of items, which each bear the name and address of a child in the class. The children are encouraged to write letters, take them to the post office, 'buy' stamps and post letters to friends in the class post box. A designated post-person distributes class letters when the class gathers on the mat. Groups of children are given a designated time in the dramatic play area. In this area they can adopt the roles of customer, recipient of a letter or parcel, post office cashier or post-person. In one hour of observing the children they use language in a variety of ways:

- *Children fill out forms and practise 'writing' official documents. They are not all able to use correct letter formation but it is noticeable that one child points out to another that you only write in the spaces on forms.*
- *Children take forms and letters to the cashier and 'buy' stamps, engaging in the ritualised conversation used in such transactions. They are remarkably aware of the sort of language used, such as 'Can I help you?' and 'I would like two first-class stamps, please.'*
- *Two children use the scales and balance to work out whose parcel is heavier. Then they experiment with rolling, rattling and shaking to work out what could be in the parcels.*

They use a wide range of mathematical and descriptive language and show quite clearly that they are thinking through their talk.

- *Several children use the paper and envelopes to make and send Christmas cards. It is clear that they know how such cards look and that they only have to write a short message in them. The children 'address' the envelopes and post them.*
- *Mrs S comes over to the post office and asks if she is in time to come and collect her family allowance money. The 'cashier' says she has just a few minutes but must hurry. She stamps Mrs S's 'book' and gives her some money, saying 'closing time now, please go out quickly' as she does it. Mrs S thanks her politely and leaves.*
- *The 'cashier' closes and tidies the post office, grumbling to himself as he does so about the untidiness of customers. He is looking at the post office from someone else's point of view. He then counts the money and writes down how many forms he has got left.*

This is a fairly typical dramatic play area. The sort of settings you will encounter include a home area, a garden centre, a space ship, a boarding kennel, a hairdressers, a toy or grocery shop, a café or restaurant, a newsagents and a supermarket. All these settings offer huge potential for literacy and oracy play. They all demand certain types of conversations and provide literacy artefacts which let children experiment with a variety of literacy acts, such as reading newspapers and catalogues and writing letters, menus, shopping lists and so on. It is important to note that Mrs S participates in the play, signalling her expectations and offering children models of language and ideas for new roles and actions.

It is not only the younger children who play with language. Word play is important for older primary children and nonsense poetry, rhymes, riddles and puns are all text types included for study, experience and enjoyment in the National Literacy Study objectives.

Practise language use

Literacy and oracy include a variety of skills that become better with practice. However, the term practice does not mean that children have to do endless, repetitive, decontextualised exercises. The use of language exercises to learn little bits of language has presented problems in the past. The chief problem is that a skill or knowledge item practised in an exercise may not transfer into the child's everyday repertoire and may not be used in other work – in which case, it is not useful to the child. Perhaps the best example of this is the child who spells a word correctly in a spelling test, then immediately gets it wrong in a piece of *extended writing*. To avoid this it is best to focus on the study of language in the context of whole texts. If a child has looked at a language element in a text and will go on to use that language element in creating a similar text, then working with it using an exercise can be useful. It is important to remember that play tasks, writing and discussion tasks in other subject areas are also good practice of literacy and oracy skills.

Develop independence

As children develop as both literacy and oracy learners they move from dependence on more experienced language learners to independence. The National Literacy Strategy recognises this and suggests a number of strategies for various levels of independence. These will probably be used each time a new text type is encountered so that children read it first with a great deal of support, explore the language of the text, write texts of that type with support and then write independently.

In planning your classroom you can also give children the opportunity to be independent learners. This means involving children in taking responsibility for organising resources, selecting activities and using the literacy resources around them, such as spelling prompts, reminder sheets and dictionaries.

Offer feedback

Having offered children clear messages about what you want them to learn, you must then offer clear feedback about their progress, both in writing and verbally. The quality of your feedback is important. If you simply praise indiscriminately, children will soon learn that your feedback does not mean much. When offering feedback about work or to questions it is important:

- **not to praise wrong answers – say they are not right and offer more support to get the answer or task right;**
- **to offer specific praise which makes it clear what has been learn or achieved, rather than general comments such as 'good' or 'well done' – ticks tell children almost nothing;**
- **to praise improvements in performance for individuals, which will not be the same as for the class as whole;**
- **to take positive feedback opportunities to look forward to the next target.**

When marking written work feedback should relate to the criteria you set for the task – either specific criteria for that task, class targets or individual targets.

Celebrate success

Finally, celebrate the literacy and oracy success of your class. One way of celebrating work is to get children to perform or read out work to the class or a group. This is also a chance to teach your children to comment positively on other children's work. Simply pointing out improvements in performance or using reward or house point charts also celebrates children's success. In literacy, high quality displays of work celebrate children's success, but remember to display the work so that others can read it. Think about the children's eye levels. Try to choose a range of achievements to display, including handwriting, composition and planning tasks as this will allow you to display the successes of a wider range of children.

The National Literacy Strategy

The *National Literacy Strategy Framework for Teaching* (DfEE, 1998) included not only the teaching objectives discussed in the introduction to this book, but also suggested teaching methods that teachers might adopt. The most significant suggestion was that children should experience a daily hour-long session of focused literacy teaching

The Effective Teachers of Literacy Project

This study was commissioned to explore how effective teachers helped children to become literate. The findings were based on a close examination of the work of a sample of teachers whose pupils were making effective learning gains in literacy and of a sample of teachers who were less effective in literacy teaching.

The research found that effective teachers of literacy tended to:

- *make it explicit that the purpose of teaching literacy was to enable pupils to create meaning using text. They were very specific about how literacy activities at the whole text, word and sentence levels contributed to creating meaning;*
- *centre much of their teaching of literacy around 'shared' texts, i.e. texts which the teacher and children either read or wrote together. Shared texts were used as a means of making the connections between text, sentence and word level knowledge explicit to children;*
- *teach aspects of reading and writing such as decoding and spelling in a systematic and highly structured way and also in a way that made clear to pupils why these aspects were necessary and useful;*
- *have developed strong and coherent personal philosophies about the teaching of literacy which guided their selection of teaching materials and approaches;*
- *have well-developed systems for monitoring children's progress and needs in literacy and use this information to plan future teaching;*
- *have extensive knowledge about literacy, although not necessarily in a form which could be abstracted from the context of teaching it;*
- *have had considerable experience of in-service activities in literacy, both as learners and, often, having themselves planned and led such activities for their colleagues.*

(Further details of this study can be found in Wray and Medwell (2002).)

(the *literacy hour*). In addition to this, they should have opportunities outside the literacy hour to hear stories, practise handwriting, do extended writing in subjects other than English, read independently and talk purposefully in a range of settings.

The literacy hour is intended to offer a clear focus on literacy teaching and to include the successful teaching techniques discussed above. The structure suggested can be summarised as follows:

- **15 minutes *shared reading and writing* with the whole class, directed by the teacher;**
- **15 minutes of focused word or sentence level work with the whole class, directed by the teacher;**
- **20 minutes of independent work for most children and 20 minutes of guided reading or writing with the teacher for selected groups;**
- **10 minutes final plenary session with the whole class.**

The *Framework* gives further details about the way these suggested time allocations use the teaching techniques discussed above. They will also be discussed in more detail in later chapters of this book. It is important to recognise that the literacy hour includes some very important teaching techniques and is one very effective way of making sure children benefit from the maximum possible teaching time as well as developing independent learning strategies. Your aim as a teacher is to make sure you use the time to include these strategies in ways that benefit children most. This does not mean that simply 'going through the motions' and producing a lesson with the right time proportions will ensure effective teaching. Effective teachers are flexible in the way they use the time — if the plenary or the whole class interaction needs to be a little longer on a particular occasion, with particular objectives in mind, then they will change the structure of the lesson. However, they do not allow lessons to lose pace or focus. Some teachers do not do the literacy hour every day, perhaps using one daily session for extended writing instead.

The literacy hour is structured so that children undertake activities that include language elements and language skills at word, sentence and text levels.

- *Word level work* includes the skills and language knowledge for spelling and vocabulary choice. This might be manifest as *phonics* activity in the 15-minute word level section of a Key Stage 1 literacy hour or as a spelling investigation in the independent section of a Key Stage 2 literacy hour. There will usually be some word level work in any shared reading and writing session.

- *Sentence level work* involves the teaching of grammar and punctuation. At Key Stage 1 this might include using punctuation to guide reading with expression in shared or guided reading. At Key Stage 2 children might do a 15-minute whole-class session on a particular grammar point which they explore further in independent work.

- *Text level work* involves knowledge about the structures of whole texts and the *comprehension* and *composition* of texts. This includes using sentence and word level skills, of course. Text level work at Key Stage 1 might include answering questions about the meaning of a story in shared reading or the author's intentions in writing this. An example at Key Stage 2 might be composing the opening paragraph of a report in the independent work section of the lesson.

The time allocations for the literacy hour are a suggestion which, when piloted across England, appeared to work well for Key Stages 1 and 2 classes. It is not intended that children working in the Foundation Stage should follow this pattern of the literacy hour in detail. These children will be learning to move from a predominantly individual type of play activity to the sort of whole-class and group activities included in the literacy hour. So, children working at Foundation Stage will probably be doing some shared reading and writing, but may do this in small groups rather than as a whole class. These children may also use whole-class time for very active, but short, activities such as phonic rhymes and phonic games. As children in the Foundation Stage develop their independence and ability to sustain attention on items they have not chosen and become used to school they will move towards undertaking a literacy hour. At the end of the Foundation Stage almost all children will participate in a literacy hour suited to their age and literacy requirements.

Effective English teaching:

a summary of key points

Key teaching strategies in successful literacy and oracy teaching include:

- *offering frequent demonstrations of reading, writing, speaking and listening;*
- *talking about language;*
- *making learning goals clear;*
- *having high expectations;*
- *encouraging the use of purposeful language;*
- *encouraging language play;*
- *developing children's independence;*
- *offering feedback on language performance;*
- *celebrating success in language use.*

Further reading

Wray, D. and Medwell, J. (2002) *Teaching Literacy Effectively.* London: RoutledgeFalmer.

Professional Standards for QTS

→ 3.3.2b

Section 3 of the Professional Standards for Qualified Teacher Status requires that you can plan, teach, monitor and assess English. This involves your being able to use learning objectives to devise effective teaching methods which will ensure that pupils achieve expected standards in reading. It also requires that you can teach appropriate elements of the National Literacy Strategy competently.

The Handbook accompanying the Standards clarifies these requirements and you will find it helpful to read through the appropriate section of this Handbook for further support.

The National Curriculum and Curriculum Guidance for the Foundation Stage

The National Curriculum for English at Key Stage I requires that pupils should be taught to read with fluency, accuracy, understanding and enjoyment, building on what they already know. In order to help them develop understanding of the nature and purpose of reading, they should be given an extensive introduction to books, stories and words in print around them.

The Early Learning Goals provide the expectation that most pupils will be able to:

- **read a range of familiar and common words and simple sentences independently;**
- **know that print carries meaning and, in English, is read from left to right and top to bottom;**
- **show an understanding of the elements of stories, such as main character, sequence of events, and openings, and how information can be found in non-fiction texts to answer questions about where, who, why and how.**

The National Literacy Strategy

The National Literacy Strategy is a text-centred programme with focused objectives at text, sentence and word level which develop language use, language study and learning through language. By the end of Key Stage I, pupils are expected to be able to:

- **read on sight high frequency words;**
- **use phonological, contextual, grammatical and graphic knowledge to work out, predict and check the meanings of unfamiliar words and to make sense of what they read.**

Introduction

This section of the book introduces you to the main features of early reading development. It discusses the kinds of knowledge children need so that they can learn to read written language, and focuses on the processes they have to become familiar with in order to be able to translate written symbols into meaning.

In the nineteenth century methods of teaching reading were conveniently divided into two main categories: they were known as the analytical method and the synthesising method. *Analytical methods* describe the process whereby the child begins by reading and understanding the whole sentence, and then focuses on individual words and letters in that sentence ('look and say' and 'language experience' methods fall into this category). *Synthesising methods* do the opposite: the child starts by building up the text, beginning with the smallest units – the letters and the sounds, and gradually working towards reading the whole sentence and longer pieces of text (phonic methods fall into this category).

RESEARCH SUMMARY

Learning to read. A simple process – or is it? The researchers explain . . .

Myra Barrs and Anne Thomas (1991) explain:

It seems that people would prefer reading to be simple: a simple and easily definable activity with simple ways of learning how to do it. But reading is not a simple activity; it is one of the mind's most complex accomplishments.

Kenneth Goodman (1976) argues that reading can never be a simple, precise act where readers decode words by paying attention to individual letters and letter blends and by recognising individual words. Instead, he asserts, readers select from the range of cues available to them (graphophonic, syntactic and semantic) and use these cues to process information.

Debates about the teaching of reading often centre around the issue of whether to teach children using a synthesising method or whether to begin by teaching whole words and sentences using an analytic method. Recently, researchers have begun to explore the nature of the reading process in more depth, and have discovered that readers use more subtle processes to get meaning from text than had previously been thought.

Reading at word, sentence and text levels

The National Literacy Strategy uses a framework in which written language is organised into different levels: *word level* (letters, blends, digraphs and words), *sentence level* (phrases, clauses, sentences, paragraphs) and *text level* (whole texts, or large portions of texts, including chapters, stories, poems, plays, reports, instructions, and so on). You need to understand how these levels operate in order to teach the literacy hour successfully.

When readers respond to a text at *word level* they use *phonic* and *graphic* cues to help them draw on two kinds of knowledge. They use *graphic cues* to help them to differentiate visually between the shapes of different letters. They use *phonic cues* to identify the sounds we use when we speak that are represented in written text by particular letters.

When readers respond to a text at sentence level they draw on their familiarity with spoken language, using grammatical or *syntactic cues* to understand the structure of written text. Children use their syntactic knowledge to predict the likely sequence of a sentence: 'he took the dog — a walk in the —', and when they learn the structure of various forms of written language – 'once upon a time', 'please close the door', 'we have painted some pictures'. Syntactic knowledge therefore helps children to anticipate word order and the words and phrases that are likely to be used in different written contexts.

When readers respond at text level they use contextual or *semantic cues* to draw meaning from the text. This meaning is twofold: it comes from their understanding of the world, and they use this to make sense of the text. It also comes from their understanding of the text itself, which gives young readers cues that help them to read new and unfamiliar words and to understand the overall meaning of the text.

The 'searchlights' model

In the guidance for the National Literacy Strategy, the knowledge and processes described above are described rather usefully as 'the reading searchlights model', with each searchlight representing a cueing system that forms a part of the reading process.

This is what the National Literacy Strategy guidance has to say:

> Successful teaching equips children with as many of these 'searchlights' as possible. Each sheds a partial light but, together, they make a mutually supporting system. The fewer the searchlights the reader can switch on, the more dependent he/she is on a single one and if that one should fail, the reader will be stuck. The more searchlights we can teach children to switch on simultaneously, the less they will need to rely on a single one and the less it will matter if one fades or goes out. Thus, successful reading is often described in terms of maximising redundancy, i.e. having as much information available from as many searchlights for as much of the time as possible. (DfEE, 1999, p.1)

Orchestrating reading cues

Word, sentence and text levels are dealt with separately in the National Literacy Strategy but, in reality, both experienced and inexperienced readers *integrate* the various cueing systems and *respond to each level simultaneously*. However, one problem that young children have as they learn to read is that they tend to use only one set of cueing systems or 'searchlights' to help them to read unfamiliar or difficult words. One child might favour graphophonic approaches and try to 'sound out' each new word, however long and complex, and risk reading so slowly that he or she loses all sense of the passage. Another child might favour using context to guess the meaning of the word. The risk here is that the child will guess wrongly, and lose the sense of the passage.

Children learn to read more efficiently when you can help them to understand the *range* of cueing systems or 'searchlights'. They can then select the cue that is most appropriate for them within a particular text or sentence, thus orchestrating their knowledge so that each searchlight or 'cue' is used to reinforce and check the others.

RESEARCH SUMMARY

'Small' and 'large' shapes
Myra Barrs and Anne Thomas (1991) do not refer to these reading processes as 'levels' or 'searchlights'. Their terminology refers to the 'small' and 'large' shapes of text. The 'small' shapes refer to words, letters and sounds; the 'large' shapes refer to a unit such as a whole sentence, a statement, a paragraph or a chapter, which carry a much greater part of the message. Can you see how these 'small' and 'large' shapes map on to the searchlights model?

RESEARCH SUMMARY

The 'interactive-compensatory model'
Keith Stanovich (1984) has proposed what he calls an 'interactive-compensatory model' of the reading process. He argues that the process of reading involves the reader in making various interactions with the text. Experienced readers who have good word recognition skills are able to concentrate more on the meaning, while inexperienced readers who have more difficulty reading individual words and phrases have to use more graphophonic cues, leaving less mental space for understanding the meaning of the text. Crucially, Stanovich argues that young readers who have little difficulty in learning sight vocabulary and in using phonic strategies often go on to be successful in their education generally, because the act of reading gives them access to a range of educational programmes that increase their general knowledge base. Those who fail in reading in the early years, conversely, lack the important knowledge that reading might have given to them.

Shared reading using a big book

You cannot assume that all young children will necessarily understand what is involved in learning to read a book. Some children will have grown up surrounded by books; others might have no experience of seeing adults reading at home, and will therefore not know how to open a book in order to find the beginning of the story. Neither will they understand that print, in English, runs from left to right horizontally along the page and is usually read from top to bottom. Furthermore, children might have no notion that the printed words that you read to them from the page of text are the same as the words that are coming from your mouth.

The literacy hour gives you an opportunity to help young readers like this develop concepts of print. Here is some general advice that you can adapt to suit the needs of particular children.

Book awareness and book handling

- Show the children the title and the cover of the book. Ask them to predict what it might be about, using the title and the cover illustration as clues.
- Talk about the author. Have you read anything else by this person?
- Talk about the illustrator. Have you read other books illustrated by this person?
- Model page turning and left–right sequencing by finger-pointing for the children.
- Encourage children to follow the text by using a pointer. If appropriate, pause before the final word as you read aloud, and invite the children, by your tone of voice, to take over the reading at this point.
- Run your finger over the letters of a word you are focusing on while you say the word slowly. Ask the children to say the whole word several times, following your finger movement. Ask the children to trace the shape of the letter in the air with their finger.

Using context

- Encourage children to respond to the illustrations by drawing attention to them and talking about their meaning in the context of the story.
- Pause in your reading and talk about what's happening, and about what might happen next.
- Focus on one particular page of the book. Encourage children to observe and talk about each character and event, using both text and illustrations.
- Encourage children to retell the story in their own words, to you and to other children.
- Encourage children to use the story in the context of imaginative role play.

Learning about words

- Point to particular words you want to draw attention to. Ask: 'What does this say?' 'Whose name is this?'
- Use a laminated sheet over the text and ask children to underline all the words on the page they know. Talk about these particular words and about any other words they are unsure of. Does the word appear elsewhere on the page? What is the initial or final sound? Are there any syllables that you can read? What does the word mean? How can we find out?
- Select a 'word of the day' from the text and encourage children to recognise and read this word in different parts of the classroom.
- Extract a longer word from the text and find any shorter words within the long word, so that the children become aware of specific letter sequences inside words.

Learning about sounds

- Fingerpoint to initial sounds or blends in words that you want to draw children's attention to.
- Run your finger, or a pointer, under the line of print as the children read alongside you. This will develop their experience of reading aloud and help them to keep together, as well as demonstrating left-right sequencing.

Guided reading

Use *guided reading* time to help children to read and interpret the text, and take the opportunity of working with a small group to show them how to use cues in order to identify new or unfamiliar words. Here are some suggestions:

- **Model page turning and left-right sequencing by finger-pointing for children.**
- **Encourage children to handle books, giving them responsibility for page-turning.**
- **Encourage the children to follow the text with their finger as you read together. Guide the child's finger if necessary.**
- **Give the child time to read to you, so that he/she feels a sense of accomplishment.**

Which texts shall I use to support these activities for shared and guided reading at Key Stage 1?

There are many texts and types of texts that are suitable for use for these activities. Here are a few criteria that might help you to make appropriate choices:

- **texts with repeated words, phrases and sentences to encourage prediction and give children the confidence to join in and follow;**
- **texts with a flowing rhythm and a language structure which helps children to predict what might happen next;**
- **texts that help children to enter the world of their imagination, so there is plenty of opportunity for them to talk about the story, to predict what will happen next, and to be excited when re-reading;**
- **texts that encourage children to become literary critics as soon as they start reading so that they get into characters' heads and judge their actions against what they themselves might have done;**
- **texts that extend children's knowledge of the world;**
- **texts with complex pictures for children to examine closely and where smaller details support the main picture and promote discussion;**
- **texts with interesting dialogue that can be read using different voices or accents e.g. *The Bad-Tempered Ladybird* by Eric Carle.**

Using environmental print to support reading in the literacy hour

Public print always has a clear purpose, whether in the form of road signs, 'danger' notices, bus destinations or advertisements. Drawing children's attention to the environmental texts around them helps them to understand that print carries a message – a crucial reading lesson in itself. We have all met children who understand very little written text in books but who can read a 'McDonald's' sign and point out 'Toys R Us' with no difficulty. By using the children's own experiences as a basis for developing their awareness of public print, you can help them to become aware of words and phrases and of the sounds within words. Here are some ideas:

- Make your own photograph book of signs around the school using a digital camera (street names, school signs, 'Way in', 'Exit', and so on). Read these regularly as your shared text and encourage children to identify particular words and phrases.
- Use carefully mounted food wrappers as an alphabet frieze round the room.
- Encourage children to make their own versions of alphabets, using everyday print such as food labels or advertisements for toys.
- Invite children to make their own advertisements for the classroom shop, or for a bring-and-buy sale. Help children to design versions of their own favourite products, using the word processor to experiment with different fonts and print sizes.
- Make a collection of local tickets and put these into a transparent photograph wallet so that children can read both sides of the tickets and talk about them together.

RESEARCH SUMMARY

The importance of environmental print in young children's reading lives

Children are familiar with a great deal of print they see around them at home and in their community before they come to school. Over twenty years ago, Goodman, Goodman and Burke (1978) already understood the value of using public print as reading material:

> *Children all seem to respond easily and appropriately to print in environmental settings. They know stop signs, the food they eat and the TV programmes they watch.*

Margaret Meek (1982) argues:

> *Public print has an important place in the lives of many young children before they come to school because it is interwoven in the daily transactions with family and community. Many a non-reader has failed just because he did not link the way he looked at advertisements on his way to school with what he has to look at on the school notice board. It is so easy for us to take all public print for granted that we often forget our part in pointing it out as something to be looked at. One of the paradoxes of being literate is that we know so well what notices and signs are, and what they say, that we no longer look at them. The learner, on the other hand, can make good use of such things.*

Hilary Minns (1987), in her study of five pre-school children, noted that they were conscious of various uses of public print: food labels, newspapers, shopping catalogues, calendars (in more than one language), advertisements, birthday cards, invitations, letters, bills, crosswords, the writing on coins and bank notes, pools coupons, diet sheets, tickets, appointments, number plates and maps.

Ann Ketch (1991) created an alphabet for her early readers based on the different sweets, drinks and savouries the children in her class chose to eat. She photographed the wrappers and put these in alphabetical order in a home-made book, which she called 'The Delicious Alphabet'. By reading the book together the children extended their knowledge of:

- *initial sounds and letters and phonic blends and alphabetical order;*
- *print styles (upper and lower case, italics, joined, etc);*
- *book handling and page turning;*
- *word recognition;*
- *prediction, and the meanings that are attached to words.*

Helping children who are 'stuck' on words: strategies to use in shared and guided reading sessions

In shared and guided reading session you will meet situations where children cannot recognise particular words. Here are some strategies to help you.

Problem	Solution
Children cannot recognise a word, even though you have read it together less than five minutes ago.	Say to the children: 'We've already read that word on page 2. Let's look at it again. Can you find where it is?' (Turn back to page 2.) Read page 2 again with the children, and finger-point as you go along, pausing at the word you want to highlight. Ask the children to say the word to you if they can, and then read the whole of page 2 again. Point to the word again and say it aloud together. Talk about anything that might help the children to remember the word – the shape, a double-letter sound in the middle, an initial letter they recognise – take your cue from them. Now return to the page you were reading and ask the children to show you where the word appears. Read the whole page, so that the word is seen and understood in context.
The children still cannot recognise or remember the word.	Stay silent for a while to give the children time to think and sort it out. (If you help too soon, the children might begin to rely on this help and not use strategies they already have in place.)
The children still do not seem able to read the word and are getting frustrated.	Tell the children what the word is (and make a note of their difficulty and what the likely cause might be).
The children read a word incorrectly but the **miscue** does not interfere with the meaning (e.g. I went to my **home** instead of I went to my **house**).	Ignore the miscue **for the time being** if you are reading a story together. The children are clearly making sense of the text and reading with meaning. At the end of the story, point out the miscue and talk about why the children might have misread the word, focusing on 'm' and 'ou'.
The children read a word incorrectly and the miscue interferes with the meaning, e.g. I went to see my **house** instead of I went to see my **horse**.	Give the children time to self-correct. If they read on without self-correcting (even though the text makes no sense with the substitution of 'house' for 'horse') talk to the children about the miscue, pointing out the significant difference between **ou** and **or**. (Make a note to reinforce the learning of these two digraphs.) Reread the whole of the sentence together. If reading 'house' rather than 'horse' changes the meaning of the text to the point of nonsense, you might want to draw the children's attention to the whole sentence or paragraph in order to help to reinforce their semantic or contextual understanding.
The children apparently read fluently, but on checking you find that they have not really understood much on the page.	Pause at the end of each page and focus on the meaning in both text and pictures. Ask questions like: What is happening here? What do you expect Joe will say on the next page? What do you think will happen in the end? Why is she looking so sad in this picture? What do you think she might be thinking? What might happen after the story ends? This will support their contextual understanding.

Problem	Solution
The children have quite a good sight vocabulary, and understand a lot of what they read, but they have very limited experience of word-building strategies.	Focus on the initial or the final sound of the word that is causing difficulty: **c-a-t** Break the word into syllables: **gar-den** Focus on the part of the word that is causing trouble: **diff-i-cult** Focus on the part of the word that the children already know: green-**house**; this might help the children to guess the complete word by using the context. Make a note of which sounds and blends are causing the trouble. Teach them separately.
The children recognise the words on the page and understand the meaning, but read aloud in a flat monotone.	Model expressive reading for the children. Read alternate pages of the text so they can hear 'the tune on the page'. Read the first sentence or paragraph on each page to give an indication of the expressive mood of the text, then invite the children to take over the reading at this point. If there is dialogue in the text, read it with the children as though you are reading a play. Give the children playscripts to read aloud in guided reading sessions. Encourage children to listen to taped stories read by experienced readers. Invite children to tape stories and to listen to themselves on tape. Talk to them about their presentation. Could they improve it? How?

Classroom story

A lesson plan for Reception children, focusing on word-level work.

The lesson plan opposite is based on the picture-story book **The Very Hungry Caterpillar** *by Eric Carle. The children already know the story because they have read it with the student several times. They have helped to make a wall frieze, painting the caterpillar, the butterfly, and all the different kinds of food it eats over the week. The student has made labels for each item of food and the children have read these on the frieze on several occasions. Now, the student is ready to attempt a more detailed analysis of some of the words in the story, matching words and pictures and focusing on initial sounds. Below is the lesson plan written by this student. As you read this lesson plan you will notice that the student has incorporated many features. Overall, the lesson has pace and a variety of stimulating and differentiated activities. Note too that the student builds in the use of a Teaching Assistant.*

Lesson: Literacy
Focus: The Very Hungry Caterpillar *by Eric Carle*

Timing	Teacher activity	Pupil activity	Reading processes and reading knowledge
Shared text work: 15 mins.	Show the front cover of The Very Hungry Caterpillar. Ask the children to join in as I read the title. Ask who the author is. Do they know anything else he has written? (Show The Bad-Tempered Ladybird.)	Children read title together and respond to questioning.	Knowledge and understanding of texts. Developing knowledge of an author and authorship in general.
	Explain that the 'phoneme thief' has struck again. The children have got to find the missing phonemes.	Children listen to instructions.	
	Read through the book and encourage the children to join in as I fingerpoint.	Children read together.	Reading text together. Following left–right sequence.
	Encourage the children to read the days of the week, following my fingerpointing.	Children read together, following finger-pointing.	Reading aloud with expression. Left-right sequencing, word recognition.
	When we come to a missing phoneme, read the word as it appears, without the initial sound. Ask the children what the word should be and then what phoneme they can hear at the beginning of the word. Ask a child to uncover the phoneme – were they correct?	Children identify the word and then say what phoneme they can hear at the beginning of it. They uncover the phoneme in the book.	Listening for initial sounds. Identifying initial sounds.
Focused word work: 15 mins.	Tell the children that we are going to play The Very Hungry Caterpillar Words and Pictures game. Arrange the children in two lines on the carpet, facing each other.	Children listen to instructions and sit on the carpet in two teams.	
	Give each child in one line a word representing an item of food the caterpillar ate. Ask each child to read it. Give the children in the opposite line a picture of the food item. Tell them that when you call out a word the child with that word has to stand up and give it to the child holding the matching picture.	Children in one team hold a picture of something that the caterpillar ate. Children in the other team hold a word that matches the picture.	Visual discrimination and word recognition. Matching words to pictures.
	Call out the name of each item of food, one at a time. After saying the word ask the child to say what phoneme they can hear at the beginning of the word.	When children hear their word they identify its initial phoneme and match it to its picture.	Phonological awareness.

Timing	Teacher activity	Pupil activity	Reading processes and reading knowledge
Activity: 20 mins.	*Show Yellow and Blue groups' activity sheet. Tell the children that they have got to find the word that begins with the initial phoneme in the picture and then cut it out and stick it in the box by the picture. Ask what the picture is and then what phoneme they hear at the beginning of 'apple'. Ask a child to find which word begins with 'a' and then cut it out and stick it in the box. Identify the other foods. Remind children to be careful when using scissors and tell them not to use too much glue.*	*Children listen to instructions.*	*Phonological awareness.*
	Dismiss Yellow group and then Blue group. Accompany Red Group to their table.	*Yellow group and then Blue group go to their tables and begin their activity.*	
	Give children in Red group their own worksheet. Encourage them to read their own sentence. Tell them they have got to find a word to match their picture to complete their sentence. Ask children to identify the initial phoneme of their picture and then find a word that begins with that sound. Then tell them to copy the sentence underneath.	*Red group read their sentence one at a time, then children identify the initial phoneme of their picture and find a word that begins with that sound. Then they copy the sentence.*	*Reading aloud. Identifying phonemes.*
	Work with Blue group. Ensure they can identify the correct word to match each picture. Ask them to say what phoneme they can hear at the beginning of each word. Then tell them to copy each word underneath.	*Blue group matches their words and pictures then copies each word. Yellow group matches their words and pictures with help from EA.*	*Word and picture matching. Word recognition.*
Plenary: 10 mins.	*Tell the children in Red group to read through their sentences. Ask children what phoneme they hear at the beginning of the food words. Ensure that Red group are standing in the wrong order. Ask the other children 'What did the caterpillar eat first, second', etc. Line up Red group in the correct order.*	*Red group read their sentences to the class. Children identify the food words and initial phonemes. Then the children remember what the caterpillar ate and Red group line up in the correct order.*	*Making a presentation to the class.*

Teaching reading at Key Stage 1:
a summary of key points

- *Learning to read is not a simple process.*
- *It involves orchestrating knowledge at word, sentence and text levels.*
- *Reading successfully involves the use of graphic, phonic, syntactic and semantic cues.*
- *Shared and guided reading are effective strategies for teaching the use of these cueing systems to children.*
- *The use of environmental print helps children make connections between reading in school and in the world outside.*
- *There are a number of strategies you can use to help children who are stuck on particular words in their reading.*

Further reading

Barrs, M. and Thomas, A. (eds) (1991) *The Reading Book*. London: Centre for Language in Primary Education.

Professional Standards for QTS

→ **3.3.2b, 3.3.7, 3.3.8**

Section 3 of the Professional Standards for Qualified Teacher Status requires that you can plan, teach, monitor and assess English. This involves your being able to use learning objectives to devise effective teaching methods which will ensure that pupils achieve expected standards in reading. It also requires that you can teach appropriate elements of the National Literacy Strategy competently.

The Handbook accompanying the Standards clarifies these requirements and you will find it helpful to read through the appropriate section of this Handbook for further support.

The National Curriculum and Curriculum Guidance for the Foundation Stage

The National Curriculum for English at Key Stage I requires that pupils should be taught the alphabet, and be made aware of the sounds of spoken language in order to develop phonological awareness. They should also be taught to use various approaches to word identification and recognition, and to use their understanding of grammatical structure and the meaning of the text as a whole to make sense of print.

The Early Learning Goals provide the expectation that most pupils will be able to:

- **hear and say initial and final sounds in words, and short vowel sounds within words;**
- **link sounds to letters, naming and sounding the letters of the alphabet.**

The National Literacy Strategy

The National Literacy Strategy is a text-centred programme with focused objectives at text, sentence and word level which develop language use, language study and learning through language. By the end of Key Stage I, pupils are expected to be able to:

- **use phonological, contextual, grammatical and graphic knowledge to work out, predict and check the meanings of unfamiliar words and to make sense of what they read.**

By the end of Year 3, Term I, they are expected to be able to:

- **identify phonemes in speech and reading;**
- **blend phonemes for reading.**

Introduction

The nature of the spelling system in the English language means that children have to learn about the relationship between the sound system and the writing system in order to read and write. This means that we have to teach children to *understand* how written text works. They do this by using different kinds of knowledge about written language: predicting meaning from what has gone before (using semantic knowledge), paying attention to the grammatical structure of the sentence (using syntactic knowledge) and learning to recognise particular words on sight (using lexical knowledge). In addition, the appearance and layout of a text gives children clues about how it should be read (using bibliographic knowledge).

Children also need phonological knowledge to support their early learning about language, both when they are learning to read and when they are learning how to represent sounds on paper. The alphabetic nature of the English language makes it imperative to use a phonic-based approach that helps young children to understand the code. Children who are taught to detect patterns of sounds in words and to relate them to patterns of letters begin to see how the spelling systems of English work and build up a foundation of knowledge for reading and writing new words for themselves. This ability gives them strategies that they can begin to use independently and it therefore builds their confidence.

RESEARCH SUMMARY

Marilyn Jager Adams (1990) carried out a major review of all the aspects of phonics and early reading instruction for the US Department of Education, and she argues forcibly for the inclusion of phonic teaching alongside other forms of reading instruction. She argues that 'approaches in which systematic code instruction is included alongside meaning emphasis, language instruction, and connected reading are found to result in superior reading achievement overall' (p. 49).

Henrietta Dombey and Margaret Moustafa(1998) also stress the importance of a good phonics programme, but argue for the inclusion of this knowledge within a whole reading programme. They argue: 'Phonics learning is dependent on experience of reading rather than being the foundation on which the whole edifice is built' (p. 13).

You will find that you can teach word-level knowledge much more satisfactorily if you create a classroom environment that supports children's knowledge of, and interest in, literacy, so a print-rich classroom provides a sound basis for learning. Here are some suggestions.

- **Create a classroom environment that is full of exciting reading material, beautifully displayed, e.g. books, posters, labels, advertisements, dictionaries, captions, notices, instructions.**
- **Use every opportunity to develop children's knowledge of the relationship between spoken and written language in real contexts (e.g. lists of children's names to do classroom jobs, displays of children's stories 'published' in the classroom for everyone to read, labels that communicate important messages – 'Please close the door quietly or you will wake the hamster up'.**
- **Choose books and other texts that support children's developing knowledge of**

sounds and letters, e.g. if you are focusing on -*at*, choose *The Cat in the Hat* by Dr. Seuss, published by Collins.

- Demonstrate writing for the children and take opportunities to write down their own words, so they begin to understand that what they say can become words on the page, and that their words are now permanent, and can be read by other people.
- Make sure you have two sets of magnetic letters (upper and lower case).
- Make a collection of rhymes and songs that help children to develop an 'ear' for rhythmic patterns.

RESEARCH SUMMARY

The debate about the nature of the reading process has always interested teachers of reading. Recent research has been sparked by the current debate about the role of phonics in the teaching and learning of reading, and this has led to a revised model of effective reading instruction (Adams, 1990). The premise underlying this model is that reading instruction should target the various elements of skilled performance: comprehension, composition, vocabulary development, word identification, rate, fluency, spelling and grammar. Furthermore, if the effects of phonic instruction are going to transfer to reading and writing performance, then we must teach skills and strategies in the context of authentic reading and writing activities. The process of reading involves coordinating information from three cueing systems: graphophonic cues (the letters), syntactic cues (the grammar) and semantic cues (the meaning). These cueing systems work together to bring comprehension from text. Many researchers believe that reading and writing development go hand in hand. Early writing activities serve to promote reading development.

The implication is that teachers should systematically integrate phonics instruction into a total literacy programme. The teaching of phonics is emphasised in the second 15-minute whole-class activity of the literacy hour at Key Stage 1, and during this time teachers should point out the purpose of phonics instruction and show young readers how they can use sound-symbol knowledge to their advantage. Likewise, one of the most important 'phonic' activities at Key Stage 1 will be writing using invented spelling – a task that involves very young children in sophisticated analysis of sounds in words.

Word-level knowledge in the literacy hour

At Key Stage 1, the National Literacy Strategy recommends that all teachers should use the second 15 minutes of the literacy hour to focus on the teaching of word-level knowledge. At Key Stage 1 this is mainly the teaching of phonics, and you need to have a firm grasp of the underpinning principles of this kind of work. These principles are:

- that the most appropriate teaching sequence in phonics goes from listening to speaking to writing to reading;
- that the concepts of syllable segmentation, rhyme and *analogy* are crucial to children's learning of the phonetic system of written English;
- that children who can recognise *onsets and rimes* are ready to move on to phonetic segmentation and the blending of *phonemes*.

The National Literacy Strategy defines phonics very broadly to include:

- **the development of the ability to recognise that speech is made up of smaller units of sound** – *phonological awareness*;
- **knowledge of the 44 sounds (or phonemes) of spoken English, and the ways in which these can be written down;**
- **graphic knowledge of the letters and letter names;**
- **the use of analogy to support reading and spelling.**

RESEARCH SUMMARY

Effective readers are able to recognise words quickly, accurately and effortlessly. How do they do this, and how have they developed this capacity? One view holds that effective readers recognise words largely through context, and that their focus on meaning reduces the need to attend to features of print (Goodman, 1976) – a strategy which, other researchers argue, slows down the process of learning to read (Stanovich, 1984). Recently, however, a very different picture has emerged. According to Adams (1990), '... deep and thorough knowledge of letters, spelling patterns, and words, and of the phonological translations of all three, are of inescapable importance to both skilful reading and its acquisition' (p. 416). Research suggests that the word recognition processes of skilled readers are so rapid and automatic that they do not need to rely on contextual information.

A teaching sequence for phonics

The teaching sequence for all word-level work in the National Literacy Strategy begins with listening activities, followed by writing, and then by reading. The components of this sequence are as follows:

Speaking and Listening
- **Support for children's growing awareness of the sounds in spoken English.**
- **Teaching children to discriminate sounds and to distinguish between them.**

Writing
- **Teaching children how sounds are represented by symbols.**
- **Teaching children to recognise and invent words with similar spellings.**
- **Teaching children to spell correctly.**

Reading
- **Giving children practice in phonemic segmentation so that they can identify words.**
- **Helping children to blend phonemes so they have a strategy for building up unknown words.**
- **Helping children to identify common patterns and analogous spellings when they read text.**

What is significant about this teaching sequence is the way in which it brings together the complementary processes of speaking, listening, reading and writing. There are wide-ranging opportunities here for you to help children to understand more about the processes involved in dealing with the alphabetical nature of the English language. You will see that you are being asked to teach children to listen for individual sounds (phonemes) in words, to read and recognise the letter or letters (graphemes) that represent the particular sound, and to write the letter or letters.

Remember, though, that children arrive at school with varying amounts of phonological experience. Some will have attended nurseries and playgroups where they have played games like I-Spy and will have perhaps been taught the sounds of the alphabet by nursery teachers or parents. Other children will have had no such experience. Baseline Assessment is designed to monitor and record such pre-school knowledge.

RESEARCH SUMMARY

Researchers tell us that children who have an early grounding in phonological awareness are more likely to become early successful readers (Goswami and Bryant, 1990). It is now well established that there is a strong connection between children's ability to detect and manipulate the sounds making up spoken words and their reading development. Phonological ability in pre-school children is one of the biggest predictors of later success in reading ability.

Word-level work in the literacy hour: learning to hear the sounds in words

When you are working with reception children, you will need to spend a great deal of time helping them to hear the sounds in words – 'educating their ears' – before you introduce them to the symbols (letters) by which those sounds are represented visually. Use the first 15 minutes of the literacy hour for activities such as these, based on your big book:

- **Spend a few minutes singing, reciting poems and jingles, and reading patterned and predictable stories, and invite children to join in.**
- **Play tapes of sounds (trains, bird song, voices, traffic and so on) to help children to 'tune into' particular sounds.**

Activities such as these will help children to become conscious of sounds in speech and in the environment – activities they will not usually have experienced as part of their everyday, pre-literate experience. Begin these activities very early in the reception class, and make sure that young children have plenty of opportunities to listen to, and join in with, rhymes and language patterns.

Learning to segment sounds

There are three levels of segmentation of sounds in words and each of these is useful in the process of learning to read. These are set out below and each will be discussed in detail:

1. Syllabic segmentation
2. Segmentation within the syllable (onset and rime)
3. Segmentation into phonemes

Syllabic segmentation

Segmentation at the very earliest stages of phonological awareness is based on the syllable. Syllables help beginning readers and writers to break big words up into manageable chunks. Most children will have some implicit understanding of syllabic segmentation when they arrive at school. Help children to increase their awareness of syllables using activities such as these:

- Ask children to clap the 'beats' in their names, e.g. Chris-to-pher, A-lex-an-der.
- Introduce children to songs or poems where they have to clap each syllable to maintain the beat (e.g. Jack/ and/ Jill/ went/ up/ the/ hill; Ma/ry Ma/ry/ quite/ con/tra/ry...)
- Make up new verses to familiar songs and clap the beats.

Segmentation within the syllable (onset and rime)

Most syllables in a word can be further segmented into two parts: the beginning or onset, and the remainder of the syllable, the rime. In the word 'mat' the onset is 'm' and the rime is 'at'. In the word 'string' the onset is 'str' and the rime is 'ing'.

RESEARCH SUMMARY

Children's awareness of the onset and rime in a syllable and their ability to manipulate these small units of language may be especially helpful for their developing literacy. Usha Goswami and Peter Bryant (1990) have suggested that children may find it easier to understand the division of words into their 'onsets' and 'rimes' rather than into individual phonemes (e.g. c-at rather than c-a-t). They have argued that it is children's ability to manipulate these units of language that may be especially helpful for their developing literacy experience. These researchers discovered that children who found difficulty in reading individual words that had a final consonant in common e.g. sat, pot, found it easier to detect these words if they shared a rime – sat, pat.

THE PLACE OF RIME IN SUPPORTING EARLY LITERACY

Many researchers into children's early literacy learning have shown that an awareness of rhyme appears to develop before children can read conventionally. Indeed, children as young as three seem to develop a fascination with rhymes and rhyming words. It's rimes that rhyme! In the literacy hour you should place a strong emphasis on the use of rhyme and you will find it very helpful to make sets of rhyming words that focus on onset and rime. The simplest kinds of words to collect are those in which the onset is a consonant, or a consonant cluster, and the rime thus contains the vowel sound plus a closing consonant. Here are some examples of the kinds of rhyming sets which would be useful to compile:

ch-ip	cl-uck	ch-ew	f-ound
d-ip	l-uck	dr-ew	r-ound
h-ip	d-uck	fl-ew	gr-ound
sh-ip	m-uck	thr-ew	s-ound

Use these words in whole-class sessions so that children have experience of listening to rhymes and predicting them. Other suggestions are:

- Complete rhyming couplets (e.g. Jack Sprat would eat no _____).
- Change the words of well-known rhymes, songs or stories so that children 'hear' different sounds and identify where they sound 'wrong', e.g.

  Mack and Bill went up the hill

  Goldisocks and the three Hairs

- Ask children to listen to the words below and to tell you which rhyme and which is the odd one out. Make up other sets of words.

bell	shell	bat	well
ball	fall	fill	wall
ring	bang	sing	wing
coat	boat	mat	goat
train	rain	chain	fun

- Ask children to listen to the words below and to say which is the odd one out this time. (Note the position of the crucial sound which varies in the words.)

bun	hut	gun	sun	(the critical sound is at the end of the word)
hug	pig	dig	wig	(the critical sound is in the middle of the word)
bud	bun	bus	rug	(the critical sound is at the beginning of the word)

Make up other sets of words.

- Ask children to select items from a box or feelie bag and to say the word for the item aloud and then find another word that rhymes (e.g. dog, cat, ball, pen, car, bike).
- Choose engaging rhyming stories to help children to become aware of rhyming words, repeating couplets, alliteration and rhythm. Some of these are:

Hairy Maclary from Donaldson's Dairy	Lynley Dodd	(1985)	Puffin
Each Peach Pear Plum	J. and A. Ahlberg	(1978)	Kestrel
We're Going on a Bear Hunt	Michael Rosen	(1989)	Walker
This is the Bear and the Scary Night	Sarah Hayes	(1991)	Walker
The Cat in the Hat	Dr Seuss	(1980)	Collins
Green Eggs and Ham	Dr Seuss	(1997)	Collins

LINKS WITH NURSERY RHYMES

The rime element of the word is used extensively in nursery rhymes. They are patterned and predictable for young readers — and are therefore very supportive because they help children to predict the parts of the word that constitute the rime. This ability helps them to develop their knowledge and understanding of letter strings and patterns in words.

RESEARCH SUMMARY

We know from the work of Goswami and Bryant (1990) that children who are sensitive to rhyme do much better at reading. A knowledge of nursery rhymes in pre-school children is strongly associated with success in reading. We also know that children who are taught about rhyme are more successful at reading than those who are not given this teaching. Rhyme, then, has to be central to any programme of phonics teaching.

Bradley and Bryant (1985) argue:

Our recommendation then is very simple. Make sure that children have every possible experience with nursery rhymes, and verses and word-games in the years before they go to school. Do everything possible to show them how the words which they speak and hear can be broken up into syllables and small sound segments.

THE IMPORTANCE OF RHYME IN HELPING TO DEVELOP LEARNING BY ANALOGY

We know that children make use of their sensitivity to rhyme when attempting to read and write new words and they do this by drawing on words they already know in order to work out unknown words, using their phonological awareness and the cognitive strategy known as analogy. This strategy involves three interlinking processes:

1. Recognising the similarity between something familiar and something unfamiliar (e.g. between a word that is known and a word that is unknown).
2. Using knowledge of the familiar item and applying it to understand the unfamiliar item.
3. Using this experience to make deductions about the differences between the two items.

Using this strategy in reading might involve thought processes similar to the following:

1. I can't read that new word.
2. I can see that the word ends in 'og'.
3. I know another word that looks like that – 'dog '
4. The bit at the beginning is different. It's an 'l'. 'd-og' is 'dog' so 'l-og' must be 'log'.

It is useful to teach children to say rhyming words like this out loud to help them to use their listening skills and phonological awareness when they are learning this reading strategy. It is also helpful to encourage them to think out loud as they go through these processes and you will need to model this for them in shared and guided reading over and over again. Thinking out loud helps children to develop explicit awareness of the processes they are going through. Invite children who are experienced in using this strategy to model this process in the second 15 minutes of the literacy hour and in guided reading time; less experienced children will then observe and hear the processes used successfully by other children, not just you.

RESEARCH SUMMARY

Bradley and Bryant (1985) argue that analogy can be used as a successful strategy in writing to develop children's knowledge of the way words are spelled:

It is probably a very short intellectual step from knowing that 'light', 'fight', 'sight' and 'tight' all end in the same sound, to understanding that that is why they all share a common spelling pattern (p. 7).

The advantages of using *analogy* are threefold:

- it makes use of children's existing knowledge;
- it helps a 'natural' set of thought processes to become familiar to fluent as well as beginning readers and writers;
- it gives access to words that you cannot analyse (break down) or synthesise (build up) by simple letter to sound correspondences.

USING ALLITERATION OR ONSETS: LEARNING ABOUT INITIAL SOUNDS

Alliteration – the repetition of words that begin with the same sound, a device used frequently in poetry – is developed by manipulating the onset unit of words, and there is evidence too that it might also be basic to phonological processing. The identification of onsets is valuable for young readers and writers because onsets or initial sounds of words and syllables give them an immediate focus when reading and writing a word. The third segmentation process is drawn from this principle.

Segmentation into phonemes

Children usually only become aware of individual sounds within words when they have begun to learn to read. The critical skill they have to learn is phonemic awareness – we have to teach them to listen for individual sounds and patterns of sounds in words and syllables. Phonological awareness, as we have seen, is to do with listening to these sounds before trying to make a link between sounds and their written symbols. Here are some ideas that will help children to focus on listening to initial sounds in words:

- **Model the learning process for the child**, e.g. 'Your name is Harry. Can you hear the 'h' sound at the beginning of your name? Let's say it together.'
- **Reinforce the child's knowledge**, e.g. 'Do you know any other names that begin with 'h'?'
- **Have some fun with sentences based on alliteration**, e.g.

    Peter Piper picked a peck of pickled peppers.

    Harry the Hedgehog has holes in his hat.

    Gertie the Goldfish has glue on her gills.

    Peter the Puma has paint on his paws.
- **Play I-Spy.**
- **Use classroom objects to reinforce understanding:**

    Point to the Lego and say: 'I can see something and it begins with le..'

    Point to the table and say: 'I can see something and it begins with ta..'
- **Use riddles:**

    You sleep in it and it begins with 'b'.

    You watch it and it begins with 't'.

    You drink out of it and it begins with 'c'.
- **Read out a set of four words and ask the question: 'Which word begins with the same sound as 'mat'?'**

    cat   chair   man   pot

MATCHING LETTERS TO SOUNDS

Children who can hear that 'dog', 'duck' and 'dinosaur' all start with the same sound (the phoneme 'd') and that 'hat', 'rabbit' and 'pot' all end in the same sound (the phoneme 't') are obviously developing an 'ear' for sounds. They might at this stage be able to notice that these words, when written down for them to see, have letters in common. As soon as you feel that children can hear sounds in words you can begin to show them how to match these sounds to their written symbols, by helping them to identify letters by the most common sounds they make. Here are some suggested activities to use at this stage:

- Introduce the words 'letter' and 'word'. Children need to know these because they will give them a consistent way of talking about a particular sound when they are reading or writing a word.
- Use the alliterative sentences above (Peter Piper etc.) in the second 15 minutes of the literacy hour and in guided reading time to highlight initial sounds with their letters. Make the sentences into posters and ask the children to illustrate them or write them on the board and then circle all the words that contain, for example, a letter 'p'. Read the words in each sentence together, finger-pointing to each initial letter.
- Recite the rhyme Wee Willie Winkie, encouraging the children to join in. If you have an illustration of Wee Willie Winkie, talk about what he is doing. Read through the rhyme again and ask the children to listen to the 'w' sounds as you read. Do they notice anything about the sounds in Wee Willie Winkie's name? Show them the verse and read it together, finger-pointing to the name of the character. Ask the children if they know any more names beginning with 'w'. Write these down, pointing to the 'w' each time.

  Wee Willie Winkie runs through the town,
  Upstairs and downstairs in his nightgown.
  Rapping at the window, crying through the lock,
  Are the children fast asleep, it's past eight o'clock?

- Use other rhymes where the central character has two names that begin with the same sound, e.g. Gregory Griggs, Sulky Sue, Mary, Mary, Charley, Charley, Jumping Joan (see The Oxford Book of Nursery Rhymes for these and other examples).
- Make collections of objects and/or words beginning with the sound you are introducing and display these. Make labels for each name and read these together, finger-pointing to the initial sound and its letter.
- Draw children's attention to individual letters in the course of sharing books, e.g. draw attention to the letter 'b' if you are reading The Three Bears. Ask the children to bring their teddy bears to school to show everyone. Make a large bear from boxes and fabrics and mount it on the display board. Ask the children to paint and then cut out (with assistance if necessary) several large letter 'b's to put round the bear. They can trace around each letter shape with their finger or in the air. Make the home corner into a Three Bears' cottage, with labels emphasising 'b's. Share stories and rhymes about bears and make a display of books about bears.

- Use easily-recognised food wrappers to reinforce knowledge of initial sounds and letters. Then prepare a list of well-known brands with their initial letters missing (-ars, -ounty, -itkat, and so on). Point to each word and ask the children to name the missing letter. Write this in the space and read the word again with the children, pointing to the initial letter, emphasising it as you read the word together.

The writing system and phonemic awareness

When children learn to write they also begin experimenting with ways of representing sounds on paper. This experimentation plays an important part in helping emergent writers to learn about the letter–sound relationships in words. Indeed, for some children this is the main way in which they will learn to become aware of the relationship between sounds and the letters that represent those sounds.

Writing and spelling introduce children to the alphabetical principle. You have an opportunity to focus their attention on letter order, letter sounds and letter shapes in order to reinforce letter-sound correspondences. This knowledge is important because, as we have seen, it is the application of spelling-sound correspondences that helps children to develop the ability to read new words, process letter sequences and develop letter-strings from these sequences. Children will begin to see the relationship between the spoken word and the written word.

Here is one idea based on a well-loved story. Use *Rosie's Walk* (Pat Hutchins) as your main text. Read the story and then say: 'Rosie is being chased by the fox. Let's say the word 'fox' out loud. Now *you* say 'fox'. Listen to the first sound of the word. Now write down the first letter of 'fox' on your whiteboards.' When the children have done this, model writing 'f' yourself for them, using the correct handwriting formation.

Teaching about blends and digraphs

Once children have a good understanding of the relationship between individual sounds and their written symbols, they can begin to run letter sounds together to make a word. The whole-class setting creates an opportunity for you to model this practice. At first you should concentrate on simple three-letter words which follow the consonant-vowel-consonant pattern (CVC words). Use the following model:

1. *I want to write the word 'big'.*
2. *What is the first sound you can hear? What is the name of its letter? How do we write the letter?*
3. *What is the middle sound you can hear? What is the name of its letter? How do we write the letter?*
4. *What is the last sound you can hear? What is the name of its letter? How do we write the letter?*

Then, having written 'big', introduce other words from the same rhyming set and show how you can write these related words by analogy. Ask children to generate and write other similar words. You might explain this as follows:

1. Now listen to this word – 'pig'. Can anyone tell me which word it is like?
2. Remember the word we just wrote – 'big'. Listen carefully to these two words – 'pig', 'big'. Are these the same or different?
3. Can anyone tell me what is different about them? (It's the beginning.) In 'big' the beginning is 'b' but in pig the beginning is 'p'.
4. How can we write the 'p' sound?
5. Then what else do we need to write to make 'pig'? Remember how we wrote 'big'?

Obviously, the more you can involve the children in thinking through this process for themselves, the better. Use the same process to introduce other words in the same rhyming set – 'wig', 'jig', 'fig', etc. On other occasions you can use different rhyming sets for this activity.

You might want to reinforce the words you have taught by using short rhymes with the children, such as:

> I used to have a pig,
> But he wasn't very big.
> He couldn't give a fig.
> What a pig!

Tap out the number of sounds you hear in a word e.g. p-i-g. Use other regular three-letter consonant-vowel-consonant words for this activity (e.g. dog, pan, sit, big, bag).

Once children can identify three-letter sequences they have made an important step towards acquiring essential skills in phonic reading. Once they have learned initial sounds and the consonant *blends* and *digraphs* which can form the initial sounds (*ch*, *th*, *sh*, *wh*) in Reception and Year 1, your phonics programme can move on to teaching long vowel phonemes and the various ways in which these are spelt (Year 1 and Year 2). The important groups to teach are:

- **Words with initial consonant clusters e.g. *bl*, *cr*, *tr*, *str*, etc.**
- **Some long vowel phonemes, e.g. seed, rain, boat, etc. (There is an opportunity at this stage for you to teach children that the same long vowel sound can be spelled by using different letters or combinations of letters (e.g. the long 'a' phoneme in 'day', 'rain' and 'cake'.)**
- **Further long vowel phonemes, e.g. oo as in 'good', *ar*, *oy*, *ow*. (As in the previous stage, teach children that the same phoneme can be spelled by different letter combinations, e.g. 'cow' and 'out'.)**
- **Further vowel digraphs, e.g. there (pronounced 'air'), law (pronounced or), fur (pronounced 'er').**

(Do be careful to take account of the predominant accents of the children you are teaching and select your example words accordingly. In some accents, for example, the long vowel phoneme in 'cone' will not sound at all like that in 'boat', and if you insist to children that these are the same phonemes, you risk confusing them completely.)

Here are some activities to reinforce this stage of children's literacy development:

- Use plastic letters to show children how to complete words, e.g. to-p, ba-t, ca-p. Help children to hear the individual sounds in blends by calling out, e.g. 'fr' and asking the children to call back 'f...r'. Do this for a few minutes in the second part of the literacy hour, using consonant blends such as *br, dr, sl.*
- Direct children's attention to digraphs. Use a picture of an animal and label it (ear, nose, eye, tail). Encourage the children to look at the word 'ear' and point to 'ea'. Ask the children to repeat it to you. Introduce them to other words pronounced the same way that use that same digraph ('near', 'fear', 'hear', 'dear', i.e. not 'bear'). Write the words so that the children can see them, finger-point to each as you say them, and ask the children to repeat them to you.
- Use well-loved books, e.g. *We're Going on a Bear Hunt* by Michael Rosen, with its patterned and predictable text. The repetition of 'swishy-swoshy' provides a perfect example of the consonant digraph 'sh' in context, and also introduces the consonant blend 'sw'. Support the children's understanding by sharing the book several times to foster familiarity with the sound patterns in different words. Point to the words 'swishy-swoshy' and encourage the children to join in with you as you say them over and over again, enjoying the sounds and reinforcing them by finger-pointing. Invite the children to join in with you. Talk about why Michael Rosen has chosen these particular words for the sound that the characters make as they walk through the grass. Ask the children what other sounds they might make if they walked through long grass, or squelched through the mud. Write these down and talk about any blends or digraphs in the children's suggestions.
- Put a chart on the wall and ask the children to write on it every time they come across a word that contains a digraph or a particular blend you are studying that week, e.g. 'ch'. (Parents can help with this activity too.) At the end of the week talk about the words the children have collected and written up, and sort them into those with 'ch' at the beginning of the word, 'ch' in the middle and 'ch' at the end. Each time you do this, you will reinforce the particular digraph or blend and enable children to reflect on the sound and to recognise words in which the sound appears.

Teaching the alphabet

Children need to be able to recognise the letters of the alphabet, in lower and upper case, and to know the letters by their names as well as by their sounds. They also need to be able to distinguish vowels and consonants and to know the order of the letters of the alphabet. Trying to learn the whole alphabet at once can be very daunting, so concentrate on just a small part to start with. Once children know the sequence of the alphabet they can begin to use it to find words in dictionaries and to use alphabetical indexes. Here are some ideas and activities:

- Use good ABC books that give the letter in the context of a word with an appropriate illustration. Point to the letters on each page, stressing the term 'letter' by saying, 'This is the letter that the word begins with...' (NB It is not necessarily helpful to tell children that, for example, 'a' is for apple. If you teach them this, do not be surprised when they write 'a' *instead* of apple.)

- Work through the alphabet a few letters at a time, pointing to and naming each letter.
- Point to the word on each page, stressing the term 'word' by saying, for example, 'This is the word apple.' Help the children to understand the relationship between letters and words by asking them to point to the first letter of the word.
- Provide opportunities for children to play with and identify wooden or plastic letter shapes. For example, put letters in a bag and ask the children to pull one out and identify it. Line the children up in alphabetical order. (NB to the first-letter place only – so all those children whose names begin with 'A' stand together. Don't at this point introduce second-letter place order.)
- Learn an alphabet song or chant to make remembering easier. Many infant children learn the alphabet to the tune of 'Twinkle, twinkle, little star'.

Phonics and phonological awareness :

a summary of key points

Good phonics teaching is essential to an effective reading programme, but only if it is embedded within plenty of meaningful text experiences.

Children need firstly to learn to hear sounds in words.

They need to learn to segment sounds, into syllables, intra-syllabic units (onset and rimes) and then phonemes.

Learning to write is an important part of learning phonological knowledge.

When children can segment sounds they are ready to be taught explicitly about phonemes, blends, digraphs, etc.

Further reading

Adams, M. (1990) *Beginning to Read: Thinking and Learning about Print*. Cambridge, MA: MIT Press.

Dombey, H. and Moustafa, M. (1998) *Whole to Part Phonics*. London: CLPE.

Professional Standards for QTS

(→) 3.3.2a-b, 3.3.7

Section 3 of the Professional Standards for Qualified Teacher Status requires that you can plan, teach, monitor and assess English. This involves your being able to use learning objectives to devise effective teaching methods which will ensure that pupils achieve expected standards in writing. It also requires that you can teach appropriate elements of the National Literacy Strategy competently.

The Handbook accompanying the Standards clarifies these requirements and you will find it helpful to read through the appropriate section of this Handbook for further support.

Curriculum Guidance for the Foundation Stage/National Curriculum programmes of study

The Early Learning Goals for language and literacy suggest that, by the end of the Foundation stage, most children should be able to:

- attempt writing for various purposes, using features of different forms such as lists, stories and instructions;
- write their own names and other things such as labels and captions and begin to form simple sentences, sometimes using punctuation;
- use their phonic knowledge to write simple regular words and make phonetically plausible attempts at more complex words;
- use a pencil and hold it effectively to form recognisable letters, most of which are correctly formed.

During Key Stage I, pupils should be taught to write with confidence, fluency and accuracy. They should be taught to differentiate between print and pictures, to understand the connections between speech and writing, and to learn about the different purposes and functions of written language. Pupils should be introduced to the alphabetic nature of writing and be taught to discriminate between letters, learning to write their own name. Pupils' early experiments and independent attempts at communicating in writing, using letters and known words, should be encouraged.

Pupils should have opportunities to plan and review their writing, assembling and developing their ideas on paper and on screen. Teachers should, on occasions, help pupils to compose at greater length by writing for them, demonstrating the ways that ideas may be recorded in print. To encourage confidence and independence, pupils should be given opportunities to collaborate, to read their work aloud and to discuss the quality of what is written. Pupils should be helped to make choices about vocabulary and to organise imaginative and factual writing in different ways.

The National Literacy Strategy

The National Literacy Strategy includes clear objectives for the development of writing, of both fiction and non-fiction. Teaching is focused around the systematic introduction of a range of text types, such as explanation, persuasion and non-chronological report.

Introduction

This chapter focuses mainly on the development of compositional skills in writing: that is, recognising who is to be written for, planning what is to be written, choosing, arranging and modifying words so that the message is conveyed appropriately. These are complex processes and yet develop at the same time as the transcription skills of spelling and handwriting. These transcription skills have their own chapter. In this chapter we will concentrate on how teachers can best support the development of writing in young children so that they become aware of the many aspects of writing and are able to manipulate written language effectively.

Development in writing

The early learning of language has been discussed in Chapter 2 but it is important to emphasise again that writing does not begin at school and cannot develop in isolation from reading and talk.

There is a great deal of knowledge about writing that experienced writers take for granted but that young children must learn. For example:

- **Adults write for lots of reasons.**
- **Other adults read what is written.**
- **What is written is the same every time it is read.**
- **Words that are spoken can be written down.**
- **What is written down can be spoken.**
- **What a word is (because there are no spaces in speech, what we refer to as a word is a unit of meaning).**
- **Print and pictures are different.**
- **Print moves from left to right in English.**

These seem like basic concepts but the degree of each child's understanding and ability when they enter school will vary. When asked what writing was, two four-year-old children, just going into school, gave quite different answers.

According to Tom, 'Writing is when you say something on paper. If someone's not there you do a letter'.

For Alexander, 'Writing is when you put the numbers in the right order to make your name'.

The Curriculum Guidance for the Foundation Stage and the teaching objectives in the Literacy Strategy present a unified progression for teaching writing and it is important that children experience this. One of the most important issues in teaching early writing is to recognise exactly what children coming into your class know and can do. This allows you to present learning to write as a continuous experience and avoid children having to cope with discontinuities of expectation. Baseline assessment will enable reception teachers to look closely at children's performance through observation and discussion. In other year groups, class records and samples of work will be passed on to give teachers a good idea of a child's development as a writer.

Children's earliest understandings about writing will be based on the experiences they have had, not just of writing, but also of speaking and listening and reading. Most children are effective speakers, although not always of English, before they come to school and it is this implicit knowledge of language they will use to develop as writers. Children whose parents read signs to them, or hold them up to the cashpoint machine, or play on the computer with them, will have given them insights into the meaning of those types of writing – signs and screen text. However, they will also have helped children make the link between the spoken and written word. When children come into school, they are able to see and hear teachers writing – doing shared writing, putting up lists, playing with children – but they are also able to talk about writing with teachers and develop a more explicit knowledge about language.

Teaching writing

The teaching of writing, building on children's existing knowledge about language, needs to:

- **engage children in purposeful writing;**
- **show children how writing works;**
- **engage children in responding to writing;**
- **encourage children to practise, explore, experiment and play with writing;**
- **give children the chance to use writing and get a response.**

Children at the Foundation Stage will work in flexible, play-orientated ways, moving towards a literacy hour as they enter Key Stage I. At Key Stage I much teaching of writing will take place in the literacy hour through shared reading and writing, guided reading and writing, independent investigations, practice activity and play. However, at both Foundation Stage and Key Stage I writing is a cross-curricular skill, which allows children to express and explore other subjects. Much of children's purposeful use of writing and practice will take place outside the literacy hour.

Shared reading and writing

Shared reading is an important demonstration, not only of the mechanics of writing, but also a chance to engage children with the ways in which forms of writing achieve their purpose. When children have read a number of traditional tales they will be able to say that stories begin with 'Once upon a time', or 'Long ago...' and end 'happily ever after'. Learning these conventions and linking them to the enjoyment of a traditional tale is the first step towards learning the structures and language use of traditional tales. Similarly, if children learn that instructions contain a number of steps to tell you what to do, they are beginning to understand how language meets its purpose. In practice, such shared reading experiences will be supported by shared writing experiences on other days. So if children have read a traditional tale on Monday and Tuesday, they may well go on to write a similar tale about a character of their own.

Shared writing involves the teacher using a flipchart, poster or overhead projector to plan, write, explore and discuss a text in cooperation with the children. Working with the whole class means that children can not only hear the teacher's views, they can also hear other children's contributions and evaluate them. As you write for children you are, of course, also demonstrating basic transcription details like writing from left to right, letter formation, use of capital and little letters, using spaces between words and working out how to spell words by sound. However, you are most importantly making the link between writing and reading and, by supporting the transcription details of writing, you are giving children the space to make language decisions such as choosing appropriate vocabulary, choosing sentence structures and word order and choosing text conventions and layout.

At the Foundation Stage, shared writing may involve a group of children or be shorter than 15 minutes. The text types will be linked to other topics in class – such as a shopping list, a description or a story. However, even at the Foundation Stage, children need a wide range of texts and to see you, a more experienced author, making text decisions.

In Key Stage I you will be able to model a number of aspects of the writing process:

- *Planning writing.* This includes a discussion of what is involved and who the piece is for, as well as children's contributions to brainstorming or making concept maps. Teaching children to plan their writing, even if only mentally, is likely to help them organise their thoughts and structures. Too many children start to write and simply keep going without monitoring the structure and effect of their writing at regular intervals.
- *Drafting writing.* Drafting may involve using a text map or writing frame to help structure the piece. You should certainly refer to any planning notes made on a previous occasion. When drafting it is important to model not only the writing down but also the sort of thinking that takes place as you decide what to write. You can induct children into this by asking for their views, opinions and reasons.
- *Revising writing.* This involves looking at a piece of writing and considering its effect and how that effect is created. This is a good opportunity to evaluate the vocabulary, sentence types, sentence structures and text features to see whether they achieve the purpose intended. By making changes on a draft you can show children that writing is provisional and can be improved. You are also showing them that there is not only one way of writing a certain text type. The editing of a piece of writing for transcription details is a very important skill, but is much less difficult for children to understand. They are usually able to look through a piece for capital letters and spelling errors quite early. They can then cope well with looking for appropriate sentence structures. Decisions about the

effect of a vocabulary choice or a choice of sentence type may be more difficult, as they are required to see the text from a reader's point of view.

When undertaking shared writing of any piece there will always be a great many features to which you can usefully draw attention. Decide which objectives you will focus on and refer back to them during the shared reading. This helps you to make clear teaching points to the children. You may find it useful to have your objectives written on a wall poster so that you can check whether you have addressed them at the end of the shared writing. When starting a piece of shared writing it is important to examine the problem – what type of text are you writing? What is this sort of text for? Who might read this type of text? What will the reader look for or expect? You may want to include this in your planning. Otherwise, planning may involve collecting and organising ideas. Planning may take a whole shared writing session and will usually involve writing notes and sentence fragments, although there will be times when you will list whole sentences. When discussing writing and language use appropriate language terms and aim to be clear and accurate. It is, of course, essential that you understand fully the text type you are dealing with and the language features you will encounter.

When drafting in shared writing you are aiming to engage and motivate all the children. It is very difficult to take contributions from a large number of children at the same time but there are a number of ways to increase participation. Some teachers use word cards or magnetic words and ask children to arrange them, which avoids the need to write at all. More usually, teachers write (or scribe) for the children. As well as scribing for a whole class, many teachers use small whiteboards for children to write words, sentences and longer passages on. They can then hold up their suggestions or show them to each other without shouting and becoming confused. Magnetic boards with letters or letter fans can be used in a similar way for spelling input. To encourage children to discuss ideas or make choices between two options you can ask them to work with a partner to discuss a language choice, but do limit the discussion time and maintain the pace of the session. When taking suggestions from children it is a good idea to ask them why they made their decision and always discuss and explain why one decision is better than another. This will help children learn how to become critical about their work as well as how to make decisions. When you are discussing issues with children it is very easy to lose the 'flow' of a piece of writing. To prevent this, always reread the preceding part of the passage when adding new material and reread the text so far at regular intervals. It is a good idea to say any proposed sentence aloud as a rehearsal before adding it to a shared writing piece. These techniques ensure that all the children can follow the writing and do not become lost and bored.

Any text type can be written collaboratively during a shared writing activity. It is particularly useful, however, in order to bring reading and writing closely together, to use shared reading texts as a starting point for shared writing. You might, for example:

- **retell together a story you have recently read;**
- **extend or finish a story you have read;**
- **rework a story by substituting a character or by changing a setting;**

- use the text you have read to 'scaffold' or 'frame' the writing, e.g. substitute new rhymes in a rhyming story (invent some new dogs to accompany Hairy Maclary, add some new animals to the story of the Grumpalump); use a simple poem to write another in the same pattern (Twinkle, twinkle, little cat ...); write a recount using a simple writing frame (First we —— then we —— Next —— When we arrived we —— Finally we ——);
- use an extract from the text as a starting point, e.g. by carrying on from opening sentences, finishing off a section of dialogue;
- write a new story round a familiar theme, e.g. new versions of fairy tales (read some of Roald Dahl's or Terry Jones' versions);
- find and record, in note form, information from the text you have read, then add further information to this.

BEFORE WRITING

- Discuss the audience for the writing – who do we want to read this (ourselves, younger children, a character in the story, the local policeman, parents)?
- Discuss the tone of the writing – how should it sound (funny, scary, informative)?
- Discuss the purpose of the writing – is it to amuse, to tell a story, to recount an experience, to give instructions, to explain, to remind, to summarise?
- Brainstorm and note down ideas for the writing.
- Discuss the sequence of the writing and how it can be made clear.

WHILE WRITING

Demonstrate and discuss:

- the difference between spoken and written language;
- the direction and sequence of writing;
- how to form sentences;
- ways of joining sentences, e.g. and, also, before, when, so;
- agreement of tense, e.g. use of past tense for narratives;
- the use of punctuation to mark sentences, speech, questions, lists;
- layout: use of titles, headings, lists, paragraphs to organise meaning;
- use of appropriate technical vocabulary, e.g. noun, verb, adjective;
- spelling strategies, e.g. building words from known syllables and letter strings, spelling by analogy from known words or word parts, referring to words in text, dictionaries and/or word banks;
- noting and investigating new spelling patterns;
- using new and alternative vocabulary for precision, to create effect, to avoid dullness and repetition;
- using expressive and powerful language;
- letter formation and consistency, upper and lower case, spacing between words;
- using other presentation features, e.g. capitals and underlining for emphasis;
- the features of different types of texts: style, grammar, language choices;
- changing writing as you work, using editing marks to indicate changes;
- adding, removing and reordering ideas;
- writing notes, asides and reminders for later inclusion or revision;
- checking for sense by rereading as you write.

AFTER WRITING

Reread the text with the class to discuss and improve its clarity, effect, suitability for purpose and audience.

Edit to improve the text – use editing marks or rewrite as appropriate.

Proof-read checking for accuracy – grammar, punctuation and spelling.

Discuss the presentation of the writing e.g. how might it be displayed and used subsequently?

Guided writing

Guided reading and writing is another intensive teaching time. Each week you will choose objectives for each group of children and some of these will be composing or sentence level objectives. Such tasks might include planning a story, character, or setting, drafting instructions or revising a text provided by the teacher. In guided writing you can undertake more detailed discussion than in shared writing and differentiate the activity more closely through support and questioning. This means that in guided writing children can often produce work of a higher standard than they would independently. In guided writing, whiteboards and magnetic boards are also very useful to share ideas and contributions. In guided writing children can produce whole-group texts, plans or revisions but this requires a high level of cooperative skills and they usually produce writing in pairs or individually. In guided writing you may use strategies other than planning, drafting and revising such as offering children sequencing passages to order or passages of writing to complete. These are useful to focus children's attention on specific aspects of language.

Independent writing

One aim of shared and guided writing is to offer children support in writing as a step towards independent writing. For every text type encountered, children need to do shared reading and writing of examples of the text type, do guided writing of selected aspects of the text and then write texts independently. This does not mean they should write a whole text in one session. In a single independent session children might plan a piece of writing or draft part of a text. The difficulty of setting independent tasks is that they must be within the child's ability range and be clear enough for the child to carry out alone. At the same time the tasks should not lack challenge. Strategies to support independent writing and differentiate tasks to suit a range of children include:

- **use of writing frames to give a writing structure;**
- **use of sentence starters;**
- **providing prompt posters for revision or text organisation;**
- **scaffolding a piece of writing by offering a range of vocabulary or ideas in the form of cards.**

The aim of these teaching techniques is to move children through a process of experiences that will help them to write independently:

- **discussing and understanding the writing task, purpose and audience;**
- **planning structures and ideas;**

- **seeing the teacher demonstrate writing;**
- **writing together with the teacher scribing;**
- **joining in composition using whiteboards;**
- **writing independently.**

The literacy hour is the main focused teaching time for writing but a great deal of writing in the early years is done as part of school routine or through play activities. The use of written instructions and signs helps very young children to make the link between reading and writing. Simple routines such as asking every child to sign in as they enter the reception class give children a purposeful writing task and, in this case, enable them to use their first secure written word — their name. Play activities are also some of the best opportunities for purposeful writing. In a home play corner, for instance, children can take telephone messages, make shopping lists and write letters, cheques and signs. To do this the appropriate materials must be available.

It is also very important that children in the early years of school have access to writing as a free play activity. This allows them to experiment with writing forms and conventions as well as choosing the purpose for their writing — such as notes to other children, pretend books or lists. To allow children to experiment, ideally, a writing area will be provided, containing a variety of papers, pencils and pens as well as attractive writing formats such as note pads and yellow Post-its. A good deal of children's experimental writing takes the form of notes and pretend letters. This will inevitably go home with the children and may not be easily accessible for you to make assessments of their understandings of writing.

A good deal of children's early writing is done in curriculum areas other than English. This has a number of advantages:

- **Other curriculum areas provide a clear purpose for writing and a ready audience.**
- **In writing outside the literacy hour there is less emphasis on children's writing.**
- **The content of writing in other areas of the curriculum is likely to be clear and may be interesting for children.**

These advantages can be very motivating for children and they can produce a huge range of text types outside the literacy hour. These include: maps, lists, reports, captions, posters, labels, diaries, word cards, instructions, accounts and many others.

Responding to children's writing

In shared writing children see the teacher as an experienced adult writer. However, the teacher is usually the child's writing audience and assessor as well.

The role of reader is very important in teaching writing because your response signals the success of the piece. It is usually possible to respond to a child's piece of writing as a reader by responding, first of all, to the content or purpose of the writing. This is especially true of unsolicited or spontaneous writing. This gives the message that the child's writing is communicative and valued. Some teachers aim to write a comment about the content of a piece of writing on each piece of work they mark.

The teacher also has a role to play as a marker and assessor of the child's work. Not all pieces of work will be marked in the same way and it is very important to mark according to the clear task criteria you have set. When possible, this should be done alongside the child, as feedback then is immediate and useful. This is not always possible, of course, and a good quality comment at a later date is better than a hurried 'good', which signifies little about writing quality or whether the child has achieved an objective.

Children learn by experimenting, and this naturally involves them making mistakes (we referred to these as 'approximations' in an earlier chapter). Mistakes should not be ignored or praised inappropriately. It is much more helpful to point out how the work can be changed and help the child to do this. When looking at a piece of work it can be tempting to focus on what the child does not know, especially features such as spelling and use of punctuation. Of course, writing conventions must be learned, and teachers should not just ignore errors, but in many cases to correct every error would destroy the work. It is more productive to look for patterns of errors.

- **Are there words or letter sequences that the child consistently spells wrongly?**
- **What is the likely explanation for a child making a particular punctuation error?**
- **Is the use of punctuation random, or does the child appear to be using a rule of some kind, even if this is not the conventional one?**

Where error patterns like these are detected targets can be set and children can improve their writing. Many teachers aim to mark one piece of writing in real detail for each half term or text type studied, then discuss it with the child in a writing conference. Some guidelines for this detailed marking will be found in Chapter 12. Conferencing then allows the teacher to probe the child's understanding about the writing processes, text types and work. It is a good time to discuss progress and review targets, which might be kept in a writing book, target file or in a home-school book. The conference also gives the teacher a much fuller picture of the child's abilities, which will contribute to record-keeping and assessment, and the piece of work and conference notes can form part of a child's portfolio of work.

RESEARCH SUMMARY

The 1980s saw a number of classic studies of young children becoming writers, notable among these being the work of Bissex (1980) and Harste, Woodward and Burke (1984). The messages from these studies are still relevant in today's classrooms and can be summarised as:

- *given access to adult models of how writing is done, many children figure out lots of the rules for themselves;*
- *adults can deliberately speed up this 'figuring out' by direct teaching, but must never lose sight of the fact that children engage in writing because it does something for them – they have the human need to communicate, and writing is just one more medium for this;*
- *looking closely at what young children write can give teachers great insight into the writing rules the children have constructed for themselves, with consequent implications for what teaching they might then need.*

Teaching early writing :

a summary of key points

- *Writing does not begin at school and most young children have ideas about it before they arrive in school.*
- *Shared writing is a powerful way of teaching all aspects of the writing process.*
- *Guided writing can provide a transition between shared and independent writing.*
- *Teachers' responses to children's writing can be a crucial factor in their engagement with the process.*

Further reading

Browne, A. (1999) *Teaching Writing at Key Stage I and Before*. London: Thomas Nelson.
Hodson, P. and Jones, D. (2001) *Teaching Children to Write*. London: David Fulton.

7 TEACHING HANDWRITING AND SPELLING

Professional Standards for QTS

→ **3.3.2b, 3.3.7**

Section 3 of the Professional Standards for Qualified Teacher Status requires that you can plan, teach, monitor and assess English. This involves your being able to use learning objectives to devise effective teaching methods which will ensure that pupils achieve expected standards in writing. It also requires that you can teach appropriate elements of the National Literacy Strategy competently.

The Handbook accompanying the Standards clarifies these requirements and you will find it helpful to read through the appropriate section of this Handbook for further support.

Curriculum Guidance for the Foundation Stage/National Curriculum programmes of study

At the end of the Foundation Stage, children should use their phonic knowledge to make plausible attempts at words and write simple regular words, use a pencil and form most letters correctly. The National Curriculum develops these abilities and demands that children use handwriting flexibly and legibly and learn the full range of spelling strategies.

The National Literacy Strategy

The National Literacy Strategy includes clear objectives for the development of handwriting abilities, including knowing when to give attention to handwriting. The Framework also sets out the range of spelling strategies and when they can be taught. There is also an additional DfEE publication (1999), *The National Literacy Strategy Spelling Bank*, which offers particularly good Key Stage 2 investigations.

Introduction

Handwriting and spelling are important parts of the complex processes of writing. One reason why these aspects of writing are so important is that they are very obvious indicators of progress. A child can easily see improvement in their own handwriting and will notice as spelling becomes easier. Developing fluency in both these areas of skill is very important as it frees attention for the other language decisions made in any act of composition. Handwriting is undoubtedly the simpler of the two skill domains and this chapter will deal with handwriting first. English spelling is complex and involves a wide range of strategies and knowledge.

Teaching handwriting

Children need to develop a number of types of handwriting:

- **a fluent, joined-up, legible everyday script;**
- **a fast, less legible hand for note-taking and making;**
- **a best handwriting which shows that they work with care and style.**

Children do not develop good handwriting by accident and all children should be doing some structured, regular handwriting practice. Schools and teachers have to decide what to teach and how to teach it.

Firstly, all children need to develop a good pencil grip and writing position. Most three-fingered pencil grips are fine, with the exception of a simple 'fist', which is not sensitive enough for writing and should be discouraged as early as possible. Fat, soft, triangular pencils encourage the development of a good grip and left-handed children should be taught to hold the pencil slightly further up the shaft, away from the point to prevent smudging. Children with severe motor impairment, such as cerebral palsy, may push the pencil through a pencil grip or airflow ball to improve control. All writers benefit from sitting at the right height with feet flat on the ground, but left-handers really need to sit a little higher than right-handers to develop a good posture.

The next priority is to learn to form letters correctly so that when children start to join up letters, the hand movements they make will work smoothly. The letter shapes of most letters in the English language are, as Sassoon (1990) points out, based on ovals and vertical lines. There is some variation for different script styles – for instance, there are several ways of forming an F, T, K, or even a letter a – but most letters are very similar. Schools in England and Wales choose a school handwriting script with agreed letter formations and joins. You must make sure that you use your school's script when modelling writing to children and that you know the differences in forma-tion for left-handed children.

Practical task

Collect an example of your 'best' handwriting, your 'normal, legible' handwriting and your note-taking handwriting. How do the samples vary in terms of:

- *consistency and regularity of letter formation and joins?*
- *orientation and consistency of spacing?*
- *proportions of letters (ascenders and descenders) and of spaces?*

These are the criteria you would use for judging the handwriting in a child's piece of writing for the Key Stage 2 Statutory Assessment Tasks.

Look at your school script. How does your writing compare to it? What changes will you have to make, and practise, for use on placement? If you are not used to writing in large handwriting on boards and flipcharts you will need to practise.

The NLS simply specifies that children should be taught correct formation of letters to facilitate joining later but does not suggest an order for the introduction of letter shapes. There are a number of ways to decide on the order of introduction of letter shapes to young children. Some theorists (e.g. Sassoon, 1990) favour particular approaches such as the introduction of letters with a similar hand movement together. In practice most teachers introduce letter formation of the letters studied in early phonics work so that children learn letter names, sounds and formation together. So most children learn initial consonants first, consonant blends and then formation of vowels. When teaching letter shapes, the emphasis should be firstly on the correct movement and only when this is achieved, on orientation, proportions relative to other letters and positioning on lines.

Ways of teaching letter formation include:

- **tracing over sandpaper letters with a finger to feel the shapes;**
- **painting big letter shapes with a paintbrush;**
- **tracing letter shapes in trays of sand or jelly with the finger;**
- **Using large letters to trace over repeatedly with crayons to form 'rainbow letters';**
- **tracing over rows of letters;**
- **using computer programs to trace letters and do letter shaped puzzles;**
- **using a finger to make letter shapes in the air or on another child's back;**
- **tracing over letters made of dots;**
- **children writing their names or tracing them.**

Some teachers use 'pencil play' activities to teach children to trace from left to right and cross the mid-line but, in practice, very few children who have had normal use of crayons and paints for drawing need these activities. Using a computer mouse is a good way of developing fine motor control but does not generalise directly to letter formation – children will still need to practise.

All these activities can be done playfully and should not last for very long – they are not particularly imaginative or stimulating and little and often is preferable to letting them become boring. These activities seek to develop habits and so really benefit from close supervision. This is a type of task where a willing teaching assistant or parent helper can make a great difference.

When children can form letters correctly they need to be taught the joins used in the school handwriting script. The order and timing of the introduction of joins is controversial. If the introduction of joins is left too late, some children have done so much printing they are unable to learn to join fluently and automatically. Some schools teach joined handwriting from the outset (as is done in France and Russia) but most schools do as the NLS suggests and introduce joining in Year 2. The NLS suggests an order for introducing joins but other orders are found in the commercially published handwriting schemes. It is perfectly acceptable to use any order the school has decided upon, as long as it is taught consistently within the school. Again, the priority in learning to join letters is correct hand movements, then neatness and proportions (in Year 3 in the NLS). As with letter formation, correct joining requires regular practice and must be checked so that bad habits are not established. Although handwriting tasks can be done in the literacy hour, they are usually quite short and do not require a

20-minute slot. Some teachers set a short handwriting task during registration and check a few children each day. Many teachers use children's drafted work as a focus for handwriting practice. Others use a commercial handwriting scheme containing exercises or passages they have prepared. There are also IT-based resources that, however useful, may not be a good use of scarce computer time unless a child has a particular handwriting difficulty.

An important aspect of learning about handwriting comes when children have to choose how much attention to give to handwriting for a particular task. In modelling writing you need to model using a fluent and legible script as well as modelling how you decide what level of neatness to use. As children become confident users of handwriting and can make decisions about font choice and presentational devices in IT, they may wish to slant their handwriting and give it a 'style'.

As children become more fluent they will learn to use ink. Biro ink is very slippery and does not help good handwriting – fibre-tipped pens are much more controllable and produce a neater result. Most children will want to try a fountain pen – it is a messy (and enjoyable) experience for most. However, fountain pen is no 'better' than any other form of ink and likely to disadvantage left-handers who tend to push the pen into the paper because of the letter-formation demands of English. Older children may enjoy experimenting with calligraphy.

A final area of handwriting, which is not primarily about motor skill, is the use of word processors to present text. Even the youngest children can use a computer mouse and some parents may have a wide range of lap-ware for the under three-year-old! Children of three, four and five can pick out letters. All children need to be taught the layout of the computer keyboard, how to highlight, underline, embolden and change fonts by Year 2 and it has been suggested that we should aim to teach children to type by the age of 11. This, however, is another (sometimes boring) motor skill to be learnt through practice and will require access to computers for all.

As with any other area of skill, some children will find handwriting easier or more satisfying than others. Unfortunately, this means some have to practise more than others. Handwriting is only a very small part of writing, and does not give a reliable indicator of the quality of the writing, so it must not always be the first criterion for marking. But remember to celebrate those who do particularly well at handwriting, as well as other parts of the writing process.

RESEARCH SUMMARY

The changes in the teaching of handwriting and spelling in the last decade have been of the some unregulated or researched experiments in recent times. In almost all schools there has been the change from a sans serif script (abc) to a script with exit strokes (abc). Sassoon (1990) points out that, by using a script with exit strokes, children do not learn a 'stop' movement which can lead to poor joining. The age at which children learn to join up has also changed. A decade ago it was usual for children to learn to join in junior school. Now, infant children routinely learn this. Peters (1985) theorises that this will facilitate good spelling because children learn to spell kinaesthetically – through habitual hand movements.

Teaching spelling

The spelling of English is complicated by the long, complex history of the language and the very flexibility of English. This means that, for the purpose of the NLS Framework for Teaching, spelling is primarily a word-level issue, but it is also partly dependent on knowing the grammar of English.

 For more information on spelling, see Chapters 3 and 4 in Primary English: Knowledge and Understanding from Learning Matters.

Practical task

Note down how you can remember to spell each word in this list correctly.

Necessary	Separate	Their
There	Unkind	Cat
Wednesday	Monolingual	Antebellum
Effect	Thought	Weir

These words use some of the strategies children must learn.

If you have completed the above task you will probably have found that there are several ways to learn spellings and that different words require different strategies.

The most obvious strategy that children can use in spelling is the use of sound–symbol correspondences to spell words phonetically. A child who can discriminate onsets and rimes can use /c/ /at/ to form a whole range of other words – bat, mat, rat, hat etc. A child who has the phonemic awareness to segment /c/ /a/ /t/ and relate them to the letters can form many more words – can, cap, cad, etc., as well as those mentioned above. This strategy may be obvious, but it is not simple.

For more information on this, see Chapter 3 in Primary English: Knowledge and Understanding from Learning Matters.

RESEARCH SUMMARY

Gentry (1982) has identified a number of stages in the development of spelling in very young children. These stages, detailed below, all indicate different levels of understanding about the spelling of English. The early stages demonstrate growing phonological and graphic awareness. Children then learn phonemic segmentation. Children who have reached the stage of transitional or correct spelling have developed the insight that sound–symbol correspondences are not enough to master English spelling and are looking at the other systems inherent in English.

Features of spelling development

1. **Pre-communicative**
   - *Demonstrates knowledge of the alphabet by forming letters to represent the alphabet.*
   - *No knowledge of sound-symbol correspondences.*
   - *Uncertain of directionality.*
   - *May mix letters and numbers, lower and upper case letters.*

2. **Semi-phonetic**
   - *Begins to match letters to sounds.*
   - *Abbreviates words.*
   - *May use a letter name to represent the whole word.*

- *Beginning to write left to right.*
- *May understand word separation and division.*

3. *Phonetic*
   - *Almost total mapping of sound–symbol correspondences.*
   - *Systematically developing spellings of certain forms such as 'ed'.*
   - *Assigns letters on the basis of sound.*
   - *Evidence of word separation and spatial orientation.*

4. *Transitional*
   - *Adheres to basic tradition of the English spelling system.*
   - *Uses vowels or vowel digraphs in every syllable.*
   - *May reverse letters due to developing visual strategies.*
   - *Draws on abundance of correctly spelled words.*

5. *Correct*
   - *Has basic knowledge of the English spelling system and rules.*
   - *Has knowledge of word structure, e.g. prefixes, suffixes, etc.*
   - *Has ability to distinguish homonyms.*
   - *Growing accuracy in use of double letters and silent consonants.*
   - *Tries out possible spelling and uses visual knowledge to select correct form.*
   - *Accumulates large spelling vocabulary of learned words.*

If you look at children's work you will notice that their early spelling does not 'fit neatly into' one of Gentry's stages but they are still very useful in helping you to infer what a child knows about spelling from what they do.

The teaching appropriate for children learning sound–symbol correspondences includes:

- **phonics teaching (see Chapter 5) in shared and guided reading;**
- **opportunities to experiment in independent work;**
- **clear, supportive feedback from the teacher which must be based on your ability to look at a child's spelling and assess what he or she knows about sound–symbol correspondences and what additional knowledge is necessary.**

The teaching of sound–symbol correspondences in shared or guided reading could include:

- **modelling and discussing children's contributions to spelling decisions;**
- **using letter fans to check which children can select letters;**
- **using whiteboards to see which children can identify letters, sequences and combinations of sounds;**
- **covering up parts of words and asking children to supply the words;**
- **highlighting letters and combinations of letters;**
- **sound rhymes and games.**

In independent activities children might develop their sound–symbol correspondences through:

- **letter games;**
- **writing for other purposes;**
- **word puzzles;**
- **making word families;**
- **sound lotto.**

As children develop as spellers they learn to use other strategies. Peters (1985) suggests that the principal mode of adult spelling is visual. Adults remember visual letter patterns as well as using sound–symbol correspondences. She also suggests that we can learn visual patterns kinaesthetically so that our hands 'get the habit' of writing certain patterns. This, it is suggested, is a good reason for teaching joined up handwriting early on. Look at the following words, for instance:

- **weir**
- **their**
- **eight**
- **weight**
- **height**
- **either**

These words are *not* a regular phonic pattern – the 'ei' makes different sounds, but they do contain a visual pattern of letters, which can be learnt through repetition. It may be worth learning these words in conjunction with handwriting practice to get them firmly memorised. The most important strategy for memorising words, developed by Peters, is known as *look – cover – write – check*. Using a paper fan or exercise book, the child copies the word, looks at it to learn the visual pattern and segments it mentally, sometimes drawing over it with a pencil or 'visualising' it in the mind. The child then covers the word up and tries to write it. If correct, then the child goes on to the next word. If not, then the process is repeated. This simple, effective strategy must be learnt by all children from Year 1 and it is helpful if all parents also know it so they can help their children learn.

One important way of remembering spellings is to break them down into 'chunks' of either morphemes or syllables. Most people remember Wed-nes-day in this way. This sort of aural learning is closely related to sound-symbol correspondences. You need to demonstrate these words in shared writing. Another type of 'chunking' is the use of morphemic analysis. If children can understand the meaning and spelling rules associated with common *prefixes* and *suffixes* they can use them flexibly. Ways to teach this include:

- **identifying words with common prefixes or suffixes in shared or guided reading or writing and discussing the meaning and/or spelling conventions associated with them;**
- **introducing the common prefixes identified in the *NLS Framework* in the whole class session and using a whiteboard or OHP to involve children in manipulating them;**

For more information on this, see Chapter 3 in Primary English: Knowledge and Understanding from Learning Matters.

- setting children a word investigation task in independent time during the literacy hour. This might include sorting words with common elements and deriving rules for their spelling and/or use.

Classroom story

Mrs B wants the children in her class to:

1. *know that the suffixes -ed, -ful, -al and -less can change words from nouns into adjectives;*
2. *know the common spelling conventions involved in adding suffixes that change words from nouns into adjectives.*

To teach this she uses the 15-minute word-level section of the literacy hour to generate lists of words which end in these suffixes. The children are then asked to focus on words that have a noun version. The class discuss the difference between 'blurred' and 'blur', 'point' and 'pointed', 'use' and 'useful' by putting each word into a sentence and comparing them.

In the independent work session, Mrs B gives children a range of investigations to complete and report back to the class.

- *One group has a set of cards with words ending in -ed. They have to identify the spelling rules for adding -ed to a word and identify which words use the suffix to make adjectives.*
- *A less able group is given two sets of words: those ending in two consonants and -ed and those ending in consonant, vowel and -ed. They have to identify the different spelling patterns.*
- *The rest of the class have similar activities with -ful, -al and -less.*

At the end of the lesson, Mrs B asks groups 1 and 2 to report their findings and makes the teaching point through their examples and findings.

Another aspect of spelling that is particularly relevant to English is word origins, or etymology. By studying the origin of a word children can learn how it is spelled. One way of finding out more about a word, and often of identifying the root of that word, is by using an etymological dictionary. This is not always simple, as most etymological dictionaries use a very large number of abbreviations. For practical purposes, a large dictionary such as the *Concise Oxford Dictionary* contains plenty of etymological information. There are also a wide range of online dictionaries and etymological dictionaries you could use. Children will also be very interested in dictionaries of place names and surnames.

There are some words we simply need to teach children to remember. Some memory tricks are those we call *mnemonics*. These tricks can help us to remember awkward words – such as 'there is **a rat** in separate' to help remember to spell it with an a rather than an e. Others include 'one **c**ollar and two **s**leeves' for necessary. These tricks can be taught to those children who have problems with particular words.

The literacy hour is usually the main vehicle for spelling study, but there is also a range of enabling strategies teachers use to offer children practice and give children independence in spelling.

To offer practice teachers sometimes set spelling tests. These can be a good learning tool or a real punishment, depending on how they are conducted.

- **The words set should either have a spelling pattern (visual or morphological) or be a set of words identified by the child for study during other writing (possibly mistakes made that week).**
- **Words to be learnt should be checked, possibly by another child, to check they are accurate.**
- **Children and parents should know the *look–cover–write–check* strategy and use it.**
- **Children who learn their spellings should achieve high marks regularly. If they do not, you may need to change the words.**
- **Children can mark each other's spellings, but you, as a teacher, should monitor achievement and intervene where a child is not succeeding.**

Spelling tests are not the main vehicle of spelling learning but can support a useful homework task and are often part of class ritual.

Strategies teachers use to enable children to be more independent in spelling include:

- **alphabet friezes and cards with pictures to help children make sound–symbol correspondences;**
- **alphabetically ordered wall 'pockets' with word cards in;**
- **word banks of topic words or common words (do make sure these are static, as mobiles are not easy to consult);**
- **a class word book in which unknown words can be written by the teacher for the child to do *look–cover–write–check* (not copy);**
- **use of an initial letter and 'magic line' to replace a word in writing so that spelling can be investigated later;**
- **a class convention whereby the child 'has a go' at a word and asks a friend before approaching the teacher;**
- **the use of dictionaries to look up spellings. This is not the primary function of dictionaries but children with some sound–symbol knowledge can use them effectively. As a teacher you should deliberately model the use of dictionaries to look up words, including the decisions you make about choices.**

As a teacher your attitude to spelling will be evident in the way you mark it. At times it will be a very important task criterion, at others it will not be the focus of marking. Some teachers mark all incorrect spellings in Year 2 and above; some only mark those they want children to learn. They feel that marking every spelling is demoralising. Each school will have a policy on this and you should adhere to it. When marking, identify words for children to learn but do not ask them to copy out the word a number of times. The best strategy is *look–cover–write–check*. When you do a detailed, thorough marking of a piece of a child's work for discussion with the child you have a chance to look diagnostically at the spelling mistakes made. Ask yourself:

- **Is there a pattern to the errors?**
- **What is causing these errors?**
- **What strategy does this child need to learn?**

In this way you can offer individual targets.

A final aspect of spelling that should not be overlooked is the recognition that some people find it easier to master the wide range of strategies necessary than others. Children who find spelling more difficult will have to pay attention to spelling in ways which the few lucky individuals who seem to 'catch' it do not. It is important that children realise they can succeed and can take responsibility for their own learning.

Teaching handwriting and spelling :

a summary of key points

- *Children need to develop a number of types of handwriting.*
- *They need to be taught correct pencil grip and correct movements.*
- *Teaching a joined writing style is now done much earlier in children's schooling than used to be the case.*
- *Fluent handwriting can assist correct spelling.*
- *There is a number of strategies that can be used to spell words, including phonological, morphological and letter string strategies.*
- *Look–cover–write–check and the use of mnemonics can be very successful approaches to teaching spelling.*

Further reading

DfEE (1999) *The National Literacy Strategy Spelling Bank*. London: DfEE.
Torbe, M. (1995) *Teaching and Learning Spelling*. London: Ward Lock Educational.

Professional Standards for QTS

(→) 3.3.1, 3.3.2b, 3.3.4

Section 3 of the Professional Standards for Qualified Teacher Status requires that you can plan, teach, monitor and assess English. This involves your being able to use learning objectives to devise effective teaching methods which will ensure that pupils achieve expected standards in reading. It also requires that you can teach appropriate elements of the National Literacy Strategy competently.

The Handbook accompanying the Standards clarifies these requirements and you will find it helpful to read through the appropriate section of this Handbook for further support.

National Curriculum programmes of study

During Key Stage 2, pupils should be taught to consider in detail the quality and depth of what they read. They should be encouraged to respond imaginatively to the plot, characters, ideas, vocabulary and organisation of language in literature. They should be taught to use inference and deduction. Pupils should be taught to evaluate the texts they read, and to refer to relevant passages or episodes to support their opinions.

They should also be taught how to find information in books and computer-based sources by using organisational devices to help them decide which parts of the material to read closely. They should be given opportunities to read for different purposes, adopting appropriate strategies for the task, including skimming to gain an overall impression, scanning to locate information and detailed reading to obtain specific information.

The National Literacy Strategy

The National Literacy Strategy includes clear objectives for the development of reading beyond the basic stages, including objectives for the development of reading comprehension in both fiction and non-fiction. These objectives include the developing ability to use text effectively as a means of learning.

Introduction

A major aim of the National Literacy Strategy has been to give all pupils as good a start as possible in their learning of literacy, and the dedication of at least an hour's concentrated teaching per day to literacy is a crucial step towards that aim. It is likely, though, that it is not in the teaching of initial literacy that the NLS has had its major impact. Teachers of Key Stage I children were usually, after all, already focusing heavily on the teaching of literacy. It has been at Key Stage 2 where the most telling changes in literacy teaching practices have taken place.

Before the advent of the NLS, there was a good deal of long-standing evidence that the teaching of literacy to children at Key Stage 2 was, on the whole, not well done. In their 1978 survey of primary schools (DES, 1978) HMI found 'little evidence that more advanced reading skills were being taught' (para. 5.30). Their 1991 report on the teaching of reading in primary schools made an almost identical statement and suggested that research such as that reported by Southgate, Arnold and Johnson (1981) and by Lunzer and Gardner (1979), for all its headline-making when published, had had little real effect on teaching practice.

HMI (DES, 1991) went on to highlight the problems which teachers of junior children had had in preparing themselves for the demands of the National Curriculum for English at Key Stage 2. The inspectors reported that in English 'too many Key Stage 2 teachers remained unaware of how far removed their current practices were from the requirements of the National Curriculum and lacked sufficient in-service training to make changes'. There appeared to be two main problems concerning the development of reading.

Problem 1: The limited range and quality of junior children's interactions with reading material of all kinds.

Narrative was very definitely the dominant *genre* both in children's reading and writing and, where efforts had been made to enhance and deepen children's responses to text, these seemed to have been confined to experiences with narratives of one kind or another. Yet it had been quite forcibly pointed out by Martin (1989), among several others, that the bulk of adult experiences with texts involved interactions with genres other than narrative. It was also the case that much of the reading done at Key Stage 2 tended to be at a surface level of understanding, rather than enhancing high quality responses in the children.

Problem 2: Children's difficulties in handling information, that is, in specifying, locating and effectively using sources of written information, for example in libraries.

There had been a long-standing concern about children's acquisition of information skills, variously referred to as library skills, research skills and study skills (Wray, 1985). The most common teacher complaint arising from this concern was usually expressed as 'How can I stop my children copying from reference books?' Although most Key Stage 2 children seemed quite aware that they should not copy from reference books, and could give a cogent set of reasons why not, when they were actually engaged in the practical tasks of locating and selecting information in books they seemed to revert to copying behaviour with little demur.

The National Literacy Strategy makes it less likely that these problems will remain as widespread. It gives a clear set of objectives for Key Stage 2 reading and suggests some important teaching strategies for developing this. Before exploring some of these, we need to look in a little more depth at the nature of what is usually referred to as *reading comprehension*.

Understanding understanding: the nature of reading comprehension

Most teachers will see a large part of their role in developing reading as being concerned with developing children's abilities to understand and learn from written materials. Often, however, views of this role have not been helped by the terms used to describe these abilities. They have been described as 'higher-order' or 'advanced' reading skills, terms which carry the implication that these skills are relevant only to the oldest or the most able children (Wray, 1981). If, however, these skills are defined as those involved in the understanding of written material, it seems clear that it is impossible to do any teaching of reading without incorporating them in some way. Understanding is, after all, the whole point of reading, and the National Curriculum sets the attainment target that children of six to seven years old should be able to 'Read a range of material with some independence, fluency, accuracy and understanding'.

Activities to develop the understanding of reading have traditionally occupied a large part of reading instruction at Key Stage 2 level. Chief among these activities has been the 'comprehension exercise', which usually consists of a passage of text followed by several questions which readers have to answer. As an example of how the comprehension exercise works you might like to try the following activity.

Practical task

Read the passage and try to answer the questions below.

The chanks vos blunging frewly bedeng the brudegan. Some chanks vos unred but the other chanks vos unredder. They vos all polket and rather chiglop so they did not mekle the spuler. A few were unstametick.

Questions:

1. **What were the chanks doing?**
2. **How well did they blunge?**
3. **Where were they blunging?**
4. **In what ways were the chanks the same and in which ways were they different?**
5. **Were any chanks stametick?**

You should have found it reasonably easy to provide acceptable answers to these questions, but you will certainly feel that you do not, even now, understand this passage. What is a chank, and what were they doing?

You are able to solve problems like this because you are a competent language user, and are able to apply your intuitive knowledge of language structures to the task. You know, for example, that the answer to a 'How well...' question will usually be an adverb (even if you do not know the grammatical term), and you also know that most adverbs in English end in '-ly'. If you can solve problems like this, there must be a possibility that primary children also can, especially as it is reasonably well established that most children are competent language users by the age of seven. This casts grave doubt on the effectiveness of comprehension exercises as a means of developing or assessing children's abilities to understand their reading.

Fortunately there are some alternative activities which can be used with children which are much more likely to involve real understanding. Some of these will be described later in the chapter, but at this point we need to look at the nature of understanding texts.

Practical task

Read the following passage which, unless you have a background in nuclear physics, you are likely to find difficult to understand. Spend some time thinking about exactly what it is about the passage that makes it difficult to understand.

Ilya Prigogine has demonstrated that when an 'open system', one which exchanges matter and/ or energy with its environment, has reached a state of maximum entropy, its molecules are in a state of equilibrium. Spontaneously, small fluctuations can increase in amplitude, bringing the system into a 'far from equilibrium' state. Perhaps it is the instability of sub-atomic particles (events) on the microscopic level that causes fluctuations on the so-called macroscopic level of molecules. At any rate, strongly fluctuating molecules in a far-from-equilibrium state are highly unstable. Responding to internal and/or external influences, they may either degenerate into chaos or reorganise at a higher level of complexity.

You probably found it difficult to understand or remember much of this passage for the simple reason that it makes little sense to you. What is it that makes it difficult?

People commonly attribute difficulty in understanding texts to the difficult words used. This passage certainly has many obscure words that do cause difficulty. Understanding, however, relies on something a good deal deeper than just knowledge of vocabulary. To see this, try the next activity.

Practical task

Read the following passage and try to make sense of it.

The procedure is actually quite simple. First you arrange things into different groups. Of course one pile may be sufficient depending on how much there is to do. If you have to go somewhere else due to lack of facilities that is the next step, otherwise you are pretty well set. It is important not to overdo things. That is, it is better to do too few things at once than too many. In the short run this may not seem important but complications can easily arise. A mistake can be expensive as well. At first the whole procedure will seem complicated. Soon, however, it will become just another facet of life. It is difficult to foresee any end to the necessity for this task in the immediate future, but then one can never tell. After the procedure is completed one arranges the materials into different groups again. Then they can be put into their appropriate places. Eventually they will be used once more and the whole cycle will then have to be repeated. However, that is a part of life.

In this passage there are no difficult words, yet it is still very hard to understand. However, once you are told that the passage describes the procedure for washing clothes, you can understand it perfectly easily.

What really makes the difference in understanding text is the background knowledge of the reader. If you have adequate previous knowledge, and if you realise which particular knowledge the new passage links with, then understanding can take place. This background knowledge can be thought of in terms of structures of ideas, or schemata. Understanding becomes the process of fitting new information into these structures. This process is so crucial to understanding text that it is worthwhile spending a little time considering exactly how it works.

Practical task

Look at the following story beginning:

The man was brought into the large white room. His eyes blinked in the bright light.

Try to picture in your mind the scene so far. Is the man sitting, lying or standing? Is he alone in the room? What sort of room is it? What might this story be going to be about?

Now read the next extract:

'Now, sit there,' said the nurse. 'And try to relax.'

Has this altered your picture of the man or of the room? What is this story going to be about?

After the first extract you may have thought the story would be set in a hospital, or perhaps concern an interrogation. There are key words in the brief beginning which trigger off these expectations. After the second extract, the possibility of a dentist's surgery might enter your mind and the interrogation scenario fade.

Each item you read sparks off an idea in your mind, each one of which has its own associated schema, or structure of underlying ideas. It is unlikely, for example, that your picture of the room after the first extract had a plush white carpet on the floor. You construct a great deal from very little information.

Understanding and, in fact, reading, is exactly like this. It is not simply a question of getting a meaning from what is on the page. When you read, you supply a good deal of the meaning to the page. The process is an interactive one, with the resultant learning being a combination of your previous ideas with new ones encountered in this text.

As another example of this, consider the following sentence:

Mary remembered her birthday money when she heard the ice-cream van coming.

Without trying too hard you can supply a great deal of information to the meaning of this, chiefly to do with Mary's intentions and feelings, but also to do with the appearance of the van and its driver's intentions – you probably do not immediately suspect him as a potential child molester. Notice that most of this seems obvious and we barely give it much conscious thought. Our schemata for everyday events are so familiar we do not notice when they are activated.

Now compare the picture you get from the following sentence:

Mary remembered her birthday money when she heard the bus coming.

What difference does this make to your picture of Mary, beyond the difference in her probable intentions? Most people say that she now seems rather older. Notice that this difference in understanding comes not so much from the words on the page as from the complex network of ideas which these words make reference to. These networks have been referred to as schemata and developments in our understanding of how they operate have had a great impact on our ideas about the nature and teaching of reading comprehension. If reading comprehension involves this kind of complex transaction between a reader's previous knowledge, ideas and attitudes, and the text, then the activities we use to develop comprehension need themselves to be interactive.

Practical task

You might want to try the above sentences about Mary on some Key Stage 2 children. Can they draw the same inferences? You might find they draw an even richer interpretation, given that they are closer to Mary in age than you are.

Experiment with varying small elements of the sentence to see what different schemata you can activate. For example:

Mary remembered her gun when she heard the ice-cream van coming.

Mary remembered her stomach when she heard the ice-cream van coming.

Interactive approaches to reading

Shared reading

At Key Stage 2, as at Key Stage 1, the first 15 minutes of the literacy hour are used to work with the whole class on a shared text. This text may be a *big book* but you might use other sources of text as well. By Key Stage 2 these shared reading and writing sessions will need to look at a wide range of texts – poems, advertisements, newspaper articles, short extracts from novels etc. Big books alone are not likely to meet the demand for such a wide range of reading material.

In any case you might not be able to use big books because the physical constraints of your classroom will not enable all the children to sit together in an area where they can all have a good view of a big book. So you will probably need to have other strategies for sharing texts with your classes. There are a number of such strategies:

- **You might be able to copy short straightforward texts by hand onto a whiteboard or blackboard.**
- **You might also make each child a photocopy of the chosen text or extract.**
- **If you have access to an overhead projector you can make OHP transparencies from the original text.**
- **You might be able to enlarge a text or extract on the photocopier.**
- **By typing a text into a word processor you will be able to print it out with a font size of around 48 point – big enough for the class to read.**

Whatever strategies you use, it is important that all the children have sufficiently clear sight of the text to read it for themselves. It is not enough in these sessions for children only to have the text read aloud to them.

You might choose to work with the same text over several days or to move each day to something different such as a text of a similar type or a further extract from the same text. The richer the text the more likely you are to want to use it for several days in a row.

A typical sequence of shared reading sessions with a Year 4 class might be organised as follows:

AIM OF THE WHOLE TEXT/WHOLE CLASS SESSION/S
- **To identify the author and title of the story.**
- **To examine the generic features of story openings: setting, characters and beginnings of plot (the who, where, when and what of the story) and consider why an author introduces these elements.**
- **To identify the use of nouns and proper nouns in stories.**
- **To identify written direct speech and speech marks.**

MATERIALS
- **Poster or OHP of the introductory page from** *The Hodgeheg* **(Dick King-Smith).**
- **Highlighter pens.**

Chapter 1

'Your Auntie Betty has copped it,' said Pa Hedgehog to Ma.
   'Oh no!' cried Ma. 'Where?'
   'Just down the road. Opposite the newsagent's. Bad place to cross, that.'
   'Everywhere's a bad place to cross nowadays,' said Ma. 'The traffic's dreadful. Do you realise, Pa, that's the third this year, and all on my side of the family too. First there was Grandfather, then my second cousin once removed and now poor old Auntie Betty...'

They were sitting in a flower bed at their home, the garden of Number 5A of a row of semi-detached houses in a suburban street. On the other side of the road was a park, very popular with the local hedgehogs on account of the good hunting it offered. As well as worms and slugs and snails, which they could find in their own gardens, there were special attractions in the park. Mice lived under the bandstand, feasting on the crumbs dropped from listeners' sandwiches; frogs dwelt in the lily pond and in the ornamental gardens grass-snakes slithered through the shrubbery. All these creatures were regarded as great delicacies by the hedgehogs, and they could never resist the occasional night's sport in the park. But to reach it, they had to cross the busy road.

SESSION 1: INTRODUCING THE TEXT
- Introduce the text to the class and explain that you intend to look at how people use writing to entertain and that this is one of the roles of a novel.
- Pick out the title and author's name and ask the children to read these with you.
- Has anyone read the book? (Don't give the story away)
- Does anyone know of other books by this author?
- If possible, show the children the actual book. Discuss the covers. Use the appropriate vocabulary – title, spine, author, illustration, blurb, ISBN, etc.
- Ask the children to predict what the book is going to be about, based on the title.
- Who might be in it? Where might it be set?
- Try to get children to say why they make the predictions they do.
- Read the extract aloud, pointing to the demonstration text, and ask the children to confirm or alter their predictions as you read.
- Check their understanding of the content:
  - Who is in the story?
  - Where is the story so far set?
  - What are the characters talking about?
  - Can children retell parts of the opening?
- Mark any unknown words with a highlighter pen and demonstrate how to look them up in a dictionary.

SESSION 2: TEXT-LEVEL WORK
- Reread the text with the class in an appropriate way. Either read it to the class or select children to read paragraphs.
- Ask the children how they know that this is the opening of a story/novel.
- Stories often try to get the reader 'hooked' straight away. Reread and underline the first sentence. What does it tell you? Did it make you interested? How? Why?
- The beginning of stories usually introduce characters. Who do they think is going to feature in this story? Highlight any references to characters.
- What do we know about the characters from this opening (characterisation)? What kinds of language do Pa and Ma use? What do we know about their family? What are their eating habits? Highlight the clues.
- The beginnings of stories often tell us where the story is going to take place – the setting.

- Where might the main part of this story take place? Highlight clues about the main setting. Does the author give us any details of the wider area (busy street, traffic, shops etc?
- A story opening often establishes when the story takes place (time of day and/or era).
- Is this story happening a long time ago or nowadays? Highlight the clues, e.g. traffic, newsagents, semi-detached houses suggests 20th century.
- A story opening also gives us some ideas about what might happen (the plot). Usually a problem arises and is solved as the story unfolds. What do we think the problem might be in this story? Highlight the clues e.g. death of hedgehogs, nice food in park, busy road and especially the last sentence of the extract.

SESSION 3: SENTENCE- AND WORD-LEVEL WORK
- Reread the text with the class in an appropriate way. Either select children to read paragraphs or ask the children to read silently.
- The story includes people, places and ideas that can be named. Pick out (and highlight) particular names (proper nouns). Note that they begin with capital letters.
- Do any of the characters speak? What, exactly, do they say? How is this indicated in the text? How do we know who has spoken? Highlight the speech marks and explain why they are called speech marks.
- Briefly recap the three sessions.
- The beginning of this story gains our attention, suggests the setting (time and place) the characters and the plot.
- Remind children of who, when, where, what.

FOLLOW-UP ACTIVITIES
- Ask the children to tell you the openings of well-known fairy stories that include who, where, when and what in the first few sentences. For example:

> Once upon a time there lived a little girl called Red Riding Hood (who). One day her mother asked Red Riding Hood to visit her Granny (who, what). Her Granny lived in a cottage on the other side of the wood (where). 'Be careful going through the wood,' said her mother. 'Stay on the path and don't talk to any strangers.' (clue to plot, what)

Guided reading and group activities

Several activities which emphasise the interaction between the ideas brought to a text by the reader and the ideas expressed by the writer have the common title of DARTS: directed activities relating to texts. These include group cloze, group prediction, group sequencing, and text restructuring, and all these activities can be used across the curriculum, not just in literacy lessons.

Group cloze

The cloze exercise consists of a text with several deletions that children have to work together to complete. The following brief example will illustrate the activity.

> John was a very lucky boy. He had been given lots of presents for his birthday and had had a ▓▓▓▓▓ birthday party. He was still rather sad, though, because the thing he had wished for ▓▓▓▓▓ all had not happened. He had wanted so much to have a real ▓▓▓▓▓ of his own; perhaps a dog, or even a cat. But Mum and Dad had said that there was no room in the flat, and John knew they were ▓▓▓▓▓. He was still disappointed, though.

The solution to these deletions lies in the combination and application of information found elsewhere in the text and in the reader's previous experiences. It also involves the application of understanding about syntactic structures. The reader has sometimes to read on past deleted words, and also to have some kind of affective response to the story. In attempting to complete the problem posed by the text the reader has to give it detailed concentration and respond to its meaning. If the problem is tackled by a group of readers, then it is even more likely that learning will take place as each reader puts forward tentative solutions and these are affirmed, questioned or extended by other members of the group.

Cloze involves much more than simple guesswork. At best it involves the systematic application of context cues, a sensitivity to nuances of meaning and to style, and the articulation of tentative hypotheses about texts. As will be seen later, it can also be a way of introducing content knowledge to children. There are a few guiding principles to its use which can help to ensure the maximum benefit.

- **Choose deletions carefully. The activity seems to work best if words are deleted on the grounds that they are likely to cause discussion. There is little point in deleting words like 'the', 'but', etc. since these generally cause little debate. It is therefore not wise to delete words on a simple numerical basis, for example, every tenth word.**
- **Leave a lead-in paragraph free from deletions. This may give children the chance to develop some feel for the style of the passage they are working on.**
- **Get children to work on the text in groups of at least three or four. They may try to complete it individually before discussing their solutions, or complete it as a group straightaway. In either case they should be told to try to achieve an agreed version as this forces them to argue for or against particular suggestions.**
- **If the children have never used cloze before, they will benefit from working as a group with you. The teacher should not supply correct answers but should rather demonstrate the most useful process of working. Procedures such as listening attentively to another's suggestions, justifying your own ideas and not being satisfied with the first solution which comes to mind can all be impressed on the children by the teacher's example.**

Group prediction

The prediction activity involves a group of children discussing, together with you, a text of which they all have a copy. The discussion should be guided by three principles:

- **Establishing purposes for reading.** The children should be reading to actually find something out, whether it be to confirm a guess as to what would happen in the text or to find evidence in the text for their opinions about events or characters.
- **Reasoning while reading.** The readers should make reasoned deductions from the information presented in the text, balancing together various facts, statements, hints and possibilities, and checking them against their knowledge of the world and its likelihoods.
- **Testing predictions.** The readers should test out predictions they make on the basis of what they read, by checking them against the actual information in the text.

In order to do these things the group are given the text one instalment at a time. As they receive each instalment they are asked to:

- **explain what is happening;**
- **predict what may be going to happen next;**
- **predict how the text will end;**
- **revise their earlier predictions in the light of new reading.**

Any comments or predictions they make have to be supported by reference to the text in front of them.

The process is thus one of shared hypothesis development and evaluation. The group are required to formulate hypotheses on the basis of what they have read and then to check these hypotheses by reference to later instalments of the text. They are involved in the anticipation/retrospection process that is at the heart of responsive reading.

Group sequencing

The group sequencing activity is based on the same principles as group prediction in that it involves a group of children formulating hypotheses about a text and evaluating these with reference to the information the text contains. It is also similar to the cloze procedure in that it involves children in checking the language they read against their own intuitive knowledge of language structure. The activity involves presenting a text to a group of children in sections, but giving them no overt clues about how the sections should ideally be arranged. The children have to rearrange the sections into an order which makes sense and which they can justify by reference to the conceptual or linguistic flow of the text. The text may be split into:

- *paragraphs*: which will focus readers' attention on the flow of meaning within a text;
- *sentences*: which will also concentrate attention on the flow of meaning, but will introduce the importance of linguistic cues, for example sequence words such as 'next', 'afterwards', or causal words such as 'therefore' and 'because';
- *lines*: which will shift attention to predominantly structural cues, especially punctuation and noun/pronoun relationships.

Text marking

Text-marking techniques, such as underlining, are used by many adults when they wish to note something in a text as being of significance. Of course, you cannot encourage children to write on school books but you can use text marking on teacher-prepared information sheets or on photocopies of pages from books. Use the strategy in a focused way with children. This can involve, for example, using different colours to mark the text in response to particular questions.

Children might also be asked to underline the sentence they think contains the main idea of a text. Different children may choose to underline different sentences and this can be used as a discussion point when children share and justify their decisions. They can also be asked to underline the most important sentence in each paragraph. Putting these sentences together should give them an outline summary of the whole passage.

Text can also be numbered to identify sequences of events. This is especially useful where steps in a process being described are separated by chunks of texts and children might lose the thread of the basic events.

Text restructuring

The essence of this strategy is to encourage children to read information and then show the information in some other way. In doing so they have to pass the information through their brain – that is, work at understanding it. Restructuring can also give you access to children's levels of understanding and thus can be a useful assessment strategy.

There are many different ways of text restructuring. Figure 8.1 shows the work produced by a group of Year 5 children who had first read a text about the process of mummification in Ancient Egypt. They marked the text to show the stages of the process and then drew a series of pictures to represent these stages. The next day, and without further access to the original text, they wrote captions to accompany their pictures.

Text restructuring can also be used with quite young children. Five-year-old Kim, for example, having been read the big book 'The life of a duck' by her teacher, showed the life cycle of a duck by means of a diagram (Figure 8.2).

Her teacher was very pleased but then asked Kim to find out how long the whole process took. Kim consulted the book for herself and then added to her diagram (Figure 8.3).

Restructuring can also take place by asking children to transpose something from one written genre into another written genre. A group of ten-year-olds, for example, had read about scribes in Ancient Egypt. Normally, perhaps, they would simply have been asked to write about what they had read 'in your own words'. This would most likely have led to a good deal of copying of words and phrases from the original text.

Mummification

1.

When someone had died they took out liver, lungs, stomach and intestines. Then they put in canopic jars.

2.

Then they took the brain out through the nostrils.

3.

They washed the body in oils and perfumes before being covered with natron.

4.

After that they wrapped the body in long linen bandages.

5.

Good luck charms were put all over the body.

6.

The mummy was then put in a coffin and buried in a tomb.

Figure 8.1 Text restructuring – 'Mummification'

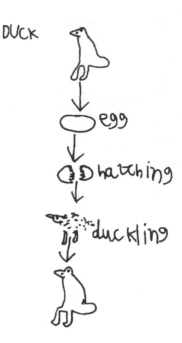

Figure 8.2 Kim's first diagram of the life of a duck

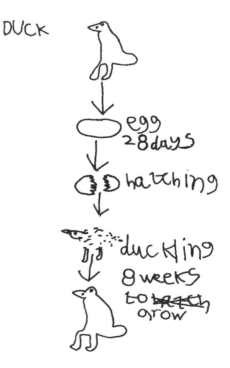

Figure 8.3 Kim's second diagram of the life of a duck

⊠ SCRIBES WANTED ⊠

Apprentices are needed to train as Scribes. Training takes 5

years. In that time you will

- learn the 700 writing signs
- practise writing
- copy letters, documents, accounts and stories
- practise division and number problems

  When qualified you will

- Collect taxes
- Keep the records/accounts
- record animals in tax counts

  Sons of scribes are invited to apply for this job. Sons of farmers
  and workers cannot apply; Training will take place in the House
  of life. Apply to the Inspector of Accounts Scribes, Egypt.

Figure 8.4 Scribes in Ancient Egypt

Greenwich

London

SA10 SM1

Mon 16 May

1547

Dear Jane

   I am heartbroken at Henry Death. He was so good to me and his children. Before we were
married I was a bit scared to marry him because he had divorced or killed 4 other wives befor me.
But he has proved me rong. I do feel sorrey for Jane Seymour because people say
If she hadnot died they would of stoied together forever. She died because she was very weak
after she had the baby. Someone made up a rime, it goes like this, divorsed, beheaded,
died, divorsed, beheaded, survived. I did love him so. The funeral is tomorrow. Would you like to
come? I will tell you how he died. I came in to check his temperature. He was
asleep. So I tried to wake him but he did not. That was when I realized he
was dead. Just Lying there pale as pale can be. Please write back.

       Written by the Royal hand of

       Catherine Parr

Figure 8.5 Catherine Parr's letter

This time, however, they were asked to rewrite the information in the form of a job advertisement. They examined advertisements in newspapers and an example of their writing is shown in Figure 8.4. As can be seen, it is unlikely that this was directly copied; instead the children had had to read and understand the information.

This 'playing around' with genres not only forces children to reorganise their material, itself an aid to comprehension, but also gives them vital experience of the variety of genre forms and guides them away from straight copying of information they have read; this is familiar to many teachers – children using factual text to provide background details for fictional accounts. Figure 8.5 shows an example of this as one ten-year-old responds to her reading about the wives of Henry VIII.

RESEARCH SUMMARY

Eric Lunzer and Keith Gardner (1979) carried out some seminal research into the use of reading among older pupils and found that the use of DARTs could significantly enhance these pupils' engagement with and understanding of texts.

David Wray and Maureen Lewis (1997) extended these ideas and explored other approaches to developing reading comprehension.

Reading for information

Classroom story

Zoe is a ten-year-old with some learning difficulties. During this half term her class is studying 'Living Things' as their topic. For this lesson Zoe and her group have been asked to choose a particular living thing which interests them and to 'find out about it'. Zoe and her friends have chosen dolphins and have picked out several information books from their class collection. For the next 45 minutes or so they work quietly and diligently with these books.

Towards the end of the lesson Zoe's support teacher arrives and goes across to check on what the girls have done. In Zoe's book she finds the piece of writing shown in Figure 8.6. She asks Zoe to read out what she has written but Zoe finds this nearly impossible to do. She also asks Zoe what she thinks she has learnt about dolphins, but Zoe cannot really think of much.

Most primary teachers will recognise what has happened here. Zoe has copied, word for word, from one or more information books. She has not processed what she has written beyond simply recognising that it is about dolphins. She has learnt very little from the lesson.

into The Blue
Of the thirty-odd species of oceanic Dolphins
none makes a more striking entrance than
Stenella attenuata the spotted dolphin.
Under water spotted dolphins first appear
as white dots against the Blue. The
beaks of the adults are white
- tipped and that distinctive blaze
viewed head-on makes a perfect
circle. When the vanguard of school
is " echolocating" on you - examining
you sonically - the beaks all swing
your way and each circular blaze
reflects light before any of the rest
of the animal. dose. you see spots
Before your eyes.

The word frenanensis comes from
the name of the artist van Bry who
drew a portraite of the type spiec
wich was stranded a bear
on the Brittany cost of France in...
the steno is in honour of the celebrated
seventeenth - century Danish anatomist
pr nuils olans steno.

Figure 8.6 Zoe's writing about dolphins

RESEARCH SUMMARY

David Wray and Maureen Lewis (1992) suggest, from their research, that most primary children know quite well that they should not copy directly from information books and many can give good reasons for this. Eight-year-old Anna, for example, told them that 'you learn a lot more if you write it in your own words'. Yet, faced with the activity of finding out from books, most children at some stage resort to copying. Why is this so common and how can teachers help children read for information more effectively?

One important part of the problem of copying seems to be the nature of the task children are often given when using information books. Zoe's task of 'finding out about' a topic is a common one but one which is not very helpful in focusing her on understanding what she finds. If the task is to find out about dolphins, then presumably any information about dolphins is acceptable. As Zoe discovers, there are whole books full of information about dolphins. How can she choose among all this information? She has no way of narrowing down the task and it becomes unmanageable. She really needs help before looking in the books in deciding what she wants to find out about dolphins.

Even if children manage to use 'information retrieval skills' well enough to locate material on the required topic, they still often find the text in that material difficult to deal with. Children in primary classrooms tend to lack experience of the different genres of non-fiction and their organisational structures (Littlefair, 1991). They find the linguistic features (vocabulary, connectives, cohesion, register) more difficult to comprehend than those of the more familiar narrative texts. Most children need support from teachers to enable them to cope more easily with the problems of factual text. There are a number of teaching strategies which can provide this support and make the activity of reading information a much more purposeful one.

What do I know and what do I want to know?

Classroom story

Zoe's support teacher did not leave things as they were. She was due to spend a lesson working with Zoe, so she decided to introduce a different way of approaching the task. At the end of the lesson Zoe had produced a very different piece of writing about dolphins (see Figure 8.7).

How had the support teacher moved Zoe on from passive copying to undertaking her own research?

The first step was to close all the information books Zoe had been using. Zoe was then asked two of the most crucial questions in the process of reading for information:

- *What do I know already about this topic?*
- *What do I want to know about it?*

The teacher scribed what Zoe said (see Figure 8.8) and together they used these questions to guide their looking in the information books.

How they live.
Dolphins live in familys and oftern there is about 7 in a family. There would be about 3 femails In one family But only one family.

1 Dolphin live for about 25 years But pillot whales can live per 50 years. Killerwhales have Been known to live longer.

Sometimes Dolphins get whashed onto the Beach which means that there skin Bodys get hot and unless they are helped Backen into the water they shall Die even if they are helped they make there way Back to help other Dolphins. They make there way Back to help Becase they hear the Distresing cry of other Dolphins. We Donot know why they Do this.

Figure 8.7 Zoe's final writing about dolphins

What I Know

clever/smart
favourite food ·squid
related to whale
live in the sea
hunted by fisherman
beautiful

What I want to find out

how they live pt8
where they live
why do people hunt them

Figure 8.8 What Zoe knew and wanted to know

There is a great deal of research which suggests that children's previous knowledge in their understanding of new knowledge is important. It is also important that this previous knowledge is brought to the forefront of the learner's mind, in other words made explicit, if it is to be useful.

Many teachers already use discussion to activate previous knowledge but there are a range of other approaches to this which have the added advantage of giving the teacher some record of what children seem to know about a particular topic. One that you will find specially useful is the KWL grid. This is a simple but effective strategy that both takes children through the steps of the research process and also records their learning. A KWL grid consists of three columns:

What do I KNOW about this topic?	What do I WANT to know about it?	What did I LEARN?

Classroom story

Zoe's support teacher introduced her to this strategy by drawing a KWL in her jotter. She then asked Zoe what she already knew about dolphins and acted as a scribe to record Zoe's responses. Not only did this tapping into previous knowledge have a vital role to play in helping Zoe comprehend the texts she was to read, but it also gave her an active role in the topic right from the beginning. By asking her what she knew, her self-esteem and sense of 'ownership' of knowledge were enhanced instead of being faced instantly with the (for her) negative experience of tackling a text without knowing quite how she was to make sense of it.

The next stage was to help Zoe establish some purposes for her reading by asking her what she wanted to know now. This helped to focus the subsequent reading.

Extending the approach

Grids such as the KWL can not only provide a written record of children's approaches to the activity of reading for information but the format of the grid also acts as an organiser, helping children see more clearly the stages of their research. It gives children a logical structure for tackling research tasks in many areas of the curriculum and it is this combination of a simple but logical support scaffolding that seems to be so useful to children.

The grid can be extended by the addition of a fourth column so it becomes a KWFL – the F standing for 'Where will I FIND the information?' An example of this can be seen in Figure 8.9 which records some of the research of a Year 5 class into Kenya.

Kenya

What do I KNOW?	What do I WANT to know?	Where will I FIND the information	What have I LEANT?
1. Kenya is a very poor country	1. How many people live in Kenya?	1. In the school Library	1. Kenya has 21000000 people liveing there.
2. Lots of crops grow in Kenya.	2. What sort of names do you have?	2. Write to the Kenya Tourist infomation Centre.	2. They have names like Rosia, Godfrey, Julias
3. They have a church	3. What is your main meal that you eat?	3. Look in an atlas.	3 Maize, yams and cassava (tropical plant like a potato)
4. They carry jugs and bowls of water on their heads	4. What sort of jobs do you have?	4. Ask Mrs Dingle	4. Ploughing, growing crops, making huts, collecting wood for the fire
5. It is a very hot country.	5. Why do women do all the hard work?	5. Ask Lisa's uncle.	
6. Everybody is black.	6. How many t.v sets do you have?	6. Look in a geography magazine.	
7. They have animals to help them grow their crops.	7. What age do people leave school?	7. In Books.	6. Kenya has over 200,000 T.V. sets.
8. Some people live in huts.		8. Leaflets.	

Figure 8.9 A KWFL grid

The grid shows that the children realised that there were more sources of useful information than merely information books and asking them to list some of these sources prompted their thinking about information. (Mrs Dingle was the fount of wisdom in the classroom who might be expected to know everything there was to know!)

Finding the answers

Locating information requires children to make decisions about where they might find the required information and then to use specific study skills such as using an index or searching a database for the details they need. The problems with this stage of the process lie not in the complexity of the skills involved but in the children's readiness to select and use the appropriate strategy to enable them to achieve their purpose most effectively. There are several ways to teach information-finding skills.

Using non-fiction big books

Key Stage I teachers are usually very aware of the advantages of using large versions of fiction texts, offering as they do the opportunity for groups of children to be able to see the text clearly, and providing the teacher with a vehicle to model how to use the features of that particular book and how to read it appropriately. Many publishers are now bringing out big versions of non-fiction books aimed at both Key Stage I and Key Stage 2 audiences and they provide a useful aid for teachers to model appropriate infor-mation-finding strategies and demonstrate a quick skim-read, scanning for a specific item of information/name and so on.

Using big books or working with a group as they undertake a research task you can demonstrate what it is you actually do – not by merely telling but by showing and accompanying the showing with a monologue of your thought processes.

Classroom story

One group of children had asked 'How long does a chick stay a chick?' Using the big book version of The Life of a Duck *('Magic Beans' series, Heinemann, 1989) the teacher modelled for the group how they might use an information book to answer their question, but as she did so she talked about what she was doing and why. She made what is usually an internal monologue accessible to the children. The conversation went something like:*

Now, Joanne asked about chicks growing into ducks. How can I see if this book has anything on chicks? What shall do I do? Shall I read it from the beginning? No, that would take too long. I could look in the index. This list of words at the back that tells me what's in the book. Yes, I can look in the index. Let's look up chicks in the index. So I'm going to turn to the back of the book. Here it is. Index. Now. It's arranged alphabetically a... b... so c should be next ... here it is. C. Can anybody see the word chick in this column...?

This kind of modelling – making explicit to the children your thought processes as you read – gives the children some very important lessons on what an experienced reader does. Explicit vocalisation of the activity provides the children with a 'learning script' which they can 'parrot' when they are trying the task for themselves. For younger and/or inexperienced learners the script often remains explicit – all teachers will have observed young children talking themselves through a task – but as they become more skilled the script becomes internalised and finally operates almost unconsciously, only being called

Simple support strategies

Extra support strategies can be used by less skilled readers or younger children in the early stages of learning to use an index and contents. Children can be encouraged to write the word they are looking for on a piece of card, underlining the first letter. Turning to the index they can then match the first letter with the appropriate alphabe-tical section before running the card down the section until they match the word.

The page numbers can then be copied from the index onto the card. This helps the child recall which pages they need to visit (they can cross out the numbers as they do so) thus helping them hold that stage of the process in their mind without having constantly to turn back to the index. Having turned to the page, the children can be helped to scan for the word by running the card quickly over the print and looking to match the word they have written. After locating the word, the children can read the sentences immediately before and after the name to see if they contain the desired information.

Developing reading at Key Stage 2 :

a summary of key points

▬ *The teaching of reading does not stop at the end of Key Stage 1.*

▬ *The process of understanding in reading is one of interaction between what a reader knows and what the author has expressed.*

▬ *There are a number of strategies to develop this interaction, including cloze, sequencing, prediction, text marking and text restructuring.*

▬ *Shared reading also has an important role to play in developing interactive reading.*

▬ *Children need to be taught to pose questions and systematically answer them when using non-fiction material.*

Further reading

Cairney, T. (1990) *Teaching Reading Comprehension*. Milton Keynes: Open University Press.

Wray, D. and Lewis, M. (1997) *Extending Literacy*. London: Routledge.

9 TEACHING WRITING AT KEY STAGE 2

Professional Standards for QTS

→ 3.3.1, 3.3.2b, 3.3.4

Section 3 of the Professional Standards for Qualified Teacher Status requires that you can plan, teach, monitor and assess English. This involves your being able to use learning objectives to devise effective teaching methods which will ensure that pupils achieve expected standards in writing. It also requires that you can teach appropriate elements of the National Literacy Strategy competently.

The Handbook accompanying the Standards clarifies these requirements and you will find it helpful to read through the appropriate section of this Handbook for further support.

National Curriculum programmes of study

During Key Stage 2, pupils should be taught to write in response to more demanding tasks. As pupils write for a wider range of purposes, they should be taught to distinguish degrees of formality in writing for unfamiliar audiences. They should be encouraged to make judgements about when a particular tone, style, format or choice of vocabulary is appropriate.

Pupils should be given opportunities to plan, draft and improve their work on paper and on screen, and to discuss and evaluate their own and others' writing. To develop their writing, pupils should be taught to:

- *plan* – note and develop initial ideas;
- *draft* – develop ideas from the plan into structured written text;
- *revise* – alter and improve the draft;
- *proofread* – check the draft for spelling and punctuation errors, omissions or repetitions;
- *present* – prepare a neat, correct and clear final copy.

Pupils should be encouraged to develop their ability to organise and structure their writing in a variety of ways, using their experience of fiction, poetry and other texts.

The National Literacy Strategy

The National Literacy Strategy includes clear objectives for the development of writing, of both fiction and non-fiction. Teaching is focused around the systematic introduction of a range of text types, such as explanation, persuasion and non-chronological report.

Introduction

When in an earlier chapter we explored the teaching of reading at Key Stage 2, we made the point that before the advent of the National Literacy Strategy the teaching of literacy to children who had passed the basic stages was especially problematic. This was particularly true with regard to the teaching of writing. Many Key Stage 2 teachers 'taught' writing principally through giving their children more and more practice at doing it. Plenty of thought often went into providing suitable stimuli for starting children off with their writing – some teachers encouraged their children to draft and redraft their writing; most took care to provide feedback to children when they marked their written outcomes. Yet the teaching of writing skills was comparatively rare. Skills in this context refer, for example, to:

- **being able to develop ideas into a form capable of being written;**
- **understanding the demands of a chosen writing form;**
- **being able to meet these demands in writing a particular form;**
- **being able to plan ahead in writing;**
- **being able to monitor, evaluate and revise what is being and has been written;**
- **understanding and meeting the demands of particular audiences for writing.**

The National Literacy Strategy details a number of teaching strategies, including shared and guided writing, through which such skills may be directly taught, and you need to be familiar with these strategies. Firstly, though, it will be helpful to clarify what we understand about the processes through which the writer has to go in order to compose effectively. (NB. We discuss the teaching of other aspects of writing, e.g. spelling, handwriting and punctuation, in another chapter.)

The writing process

Writing often seems a very mysterious process. When we write, somehow or other ideas which are in our heads, perhaps only in the very vaguest of forms, have to be shaped into coherent representations in language and transferred onto paper, screen or other media so they can be inspected by some other person. Although we vary greatly in the amount of writing that we do, we all have a tendency to take the process for granted. Even those who write a great deal will, when asked to describe the difficulties of writing, tend to focus on the original development of ideas rather than on the process of shaping these into language. The term we use to describe having difficulties in writing, 'writer's block', is understood by most people to mean having difficulty in getting ideas for writing rather than difficulty in transferring these to the page.

Yet the process of writing is not so simple. How exactly do we shape our ideas into writeable forms, and does the process then simply involve the transferring of these ideas to a page? Do we all follow the same process in writing or does the process vary according to how skilful we are at writing, how experienced we are, our individual styles or personalities, or on any other dimension?

You might begin a closer look at these questions by examining your own writing processes.

Practical task

1. **Think about the most recent piece of sustained writing you have done. Examples you might choose could be a personal letter to a friend or a policy document for your school. How did you actually set about this writing? Jot down, in note form, as much as you can remember about your approach to this task.**

2. **It would be very useful if you could compare your approach to this writing task to that of someone else. Are there similarities or differences in the ways you both tackled the task? If there are differences, how might you account for these? Are they merely the result of you both engaging in slightly different writing tasks or are there more fundamental reasons for the differences?**

You probably discerned several stages to the process of writing. The sequence below may not agree completely with your own description but might be useful as a starting point for discussion.

In order to produce a piece of writing, the writer needs to:

- **have something worth saying;**
- **decide that writing is the most appropriate medium for saying this;**
- **have an audience in mind for what will be written;**
- **think about how ideas will be expressed;**
- **put these expressions down on paper;**
- **reconsider what has been written, and perhaps make alterations;**
- **pass on the writing to where it was intended to go.**

These stages do not include the pencil sharpening, false starts, coffee making and various other activities that some writers find essential! Very few adults are able to produce a neat, accurate piece of writing that says all they want to say in the appropriate style and form at one short sitting. Interruptions and disruptions are normal in experiences of writing rather than exceptions.

Dimensions of the writing process

Our look above at the activities of an adult writer has revealed the multiple dimensions involved in the writing process. Let us look more closely at these dimensions.

In order to communicate ideas the writer must compose. This involves:

- **getting and evaluating information;**
- **evolving and synthesising ideas;**
- **shaping information and ideas into a form that can be expressed in writing.**

This is essentially a creative act involving the moulding of ideas and the creation and ordering of knowledge. *Composition* is, therefore, a thoughtful activity. This view of composition, and writing in general, places emphasis on the role of language as a means of making sense of the world. As writers write they shape their experiences and ideas in novel ways, and in the course of this usually clarify what is in their minds. Some people claim writing to be 'epistemic', that is a creator of knowledge in its own right.

The writer must also transcribe the composition. This involves choosing an appropriate form and presenting a correct layout. *Transcription* also sometimes requires attention to accuracy in spelling, grammar, punctuation and handwriting. It is clear that transcription assumes different levels of importance depending upon the purpose of and *audience* for a piece of writing. A letter to a bank manager or an application for a job requires much more care to be given to features such as spelling and handwriting than do shopping lists or the notes we take during a lecture. Yet transcription always takes place and always demands some of our attention in writing.

Ideally, the writer should be able to coordinate these two dimensions of writing, but this is often difficult. Composition and transcription may inhibit one another and orchestrating the two may be very difficult. Many adults find that they make more mistakes and changes when writing something important because their minds are so involved with composing the ideas. For children, who may have less than complete mastery of the processes involved, this orchestration is doubly difficult.

The result of this problem of coordination is sometimes that children come to believe that particular parts of the writing process are more important than others and should take the lion's share of their attention.

RESEARCH SUMMARY

As part of a study of children's ideas about writing in school, David Wray asked a large group of primary children, aged 7 to 11 years, to write a response to the following statement:

Someone in the class below yours has asked you what the writing will be like when he/she comes into your class. Write and tell him/her, and try to give him/her some useful advice about what he/she will have to do to do good writing in your class.

The children's responses were read and a record kept of their mentions of particular aspects of writing. The following list shows the aspects that were mentioned, in order of their popularity:

1. *Spelling (mentioned 579 times, that is 19.88% of the total number of mentions of all features). It would usually be referred to by phrases such as, 'Make sure you get your spellings right', or 'Use a dictionary to spell words you don't know'.*
2. *Neatness (503 – 17.27%). This would be referred to by statements like, 'Do your best handwriting' or 'Make sure it is not messy'.*
3. *Length (372 – 12.77%). Many children stressed that the writing had to be 'long enough', although a significant number warned not to make it too long 'because Miss might get bored'.*
4. *Ideas (359 – 12.33%). There were several comments along the lines of: 'Try to have some funny bits', or 'Stories should be interesting and exciting'.*

5. *Punctuation (312 – 10.71%). Here were mentions of the need for full stops and capital letters, commas and speech marks.*
6. *Words (213 – 7.31%). Statements were used such as 'Don't use the same word over and over again'.*
7. *Tools (160 – 5.49%). There was surprisingly frequent mention of the materials with which to write, such as 'make sure your pencil is sharp', or 'Mr Ellis gets cross if you do not use a ruler to underline the title'.*
8. *Structure (132 – 4.53%). There was some mention of structural features such as 'A story needs a beginning, a middle and an end'.*
9. *Characters (100 – 3.43%). Some children gave advice such as 'Write about interesting people'.*
10. *Style (60 – 2.06%). Relatively few mentions were made of stylistic features such as 'In poems you can repeat words to make it sound good', or 'Don't begin sentences with "and"'.*
11. *Layout (46 – 1.58%). Some children referred to the drawing of a margin or the placing of the date, etc.*

It seems that primary children on the whole do not value aspects of writing connected with composition but pay greater attention to transcription. This suggests that when children are writing they are likely to be giving so much attention to transcribing that they have little to spare for composition, which is arguably the most important dimension of writing. To develop fully as writers, children will need help in orchestrating the dimensions.

Breaking down the writing process

One way of overcoming the problem of orchestrating dimensions of writing is to approach composition and transcription separately with children. You might do this by introducing them to the drafting process, that is, to the idea that a piece of writing may go through several versions. This approach can allow the writer the freedom to concentrate firstly on composition and then later to deal with transcription. Drafting, however, implies more than just 'writing it in rough first'. It allows children to get to grips with three very important processes in writing: planning, revision and editing.

Breaking down the writing process in this way is characteristic of the work of Donald Graves, whose 1983 book Writing: Teachers and Children at Work *is widely regarded as having begun the 'process writing' movement. In the United Kingdom, Graves' work heavily influenced the National Writing Project (1987-90).*

PLANNING

Many children have only vague notions about planning. Elizabeth (eight years old), when asked how she planned her writing, said, 'I write the first idea, then I get another one and I write it down, and I go on until I've run out, and that's the end.' While this may be appropriate in a few situations, it is not the way adult writers work, nor is it the ideal way for children to work. Planning can help children to generate ideas and formulate thoughts. Noting down their plans for writing can also help children remember all the ideas they want to work with. Eira (seven years old) commented, 'the plan sort of helps when it brings back the ideas I forget, and I get new ones then too.' If the burden of memory is alleviated, the child may be better able to reflect upon and organise those ideas.

There are many ways to plan a piece of writing: a child may jot down a few key words from a class *brainstorming* session, they may create idea webs, or there may be a class 'formula' introduced by the teacher.

One teacher introduced her class of nine-year-olds to the idea of topic webs. They began with the topic for writing in the centre and then brainstormed connected ideas that were added to the web. This teacher taught her children that 'ideas are like butterflies; if you don't catch them quickly and write them down, they soon flutter away'.

Another teacher decided to introduce her class of seven-year-olds to planning by asking them to draw 'beginning', 'middle', and 'end' boxes and put key words into them. This focused their attention on the structure of their writing.

Another idea that has been successfully used by teachers is to give children frameworks around which to structure their writing (see Lewis and Wray, 1994 for more details of this approach). *Writing frames* provide children with sets of sentence starts and connectives into which they work their own ideas. The frame helps keep their writing coherent and can act as a plan and a set of prompts to writing.

Different frames can help children plan different types of writing. If, for example, they are reporting on research they have been carrying out using information books, they may use a frame like the following:

> Although I already knew that ....
>
> I have learnt some new facts. I learnt that ....
>
> I also learnt that ....
>
> Another fact I learnt ....
>
> However the most interesting thing I learnt was ....

If, however, they are planning to write an argument in favour of a particular viewpoint, the frame may look like this:

> Although not everybody would agree, I want to argue that ....
>
> I have several reasons for arguing for this point of view. My first reason is .....
>
> A further reason is...
>
> Furthermore...

Therefore, although some people argue that ....

I think I have shown that ....

Many children will need this sort of help to get started, but it is important that through their school careers they experience planning in different ways, for two main reasons. Firstly, some types of planning, like the examples above, help develop certain features only of writing. More importantly, though, you are aiming to give children sufficient experience to enable them to choose a form of planning most suited to their needs. The form and amount of planning necessary depends on the child and on the task.

REVISION

If children are allowed to draft work they are more likely to see it as provisional, and therefore change and improve it. Children, and adults, may need to reflect upon and revise their compositions several times.

It is important to realise the difference between *revision* and *editing*. Revision implies qualitative change of content, style or sequence. Although it is the most difficult aspect of the writing process to introduce, revision of drafted writing should naturally follow on from planning. The questions writers ask themselves during revision will depend on the piece of writing, but will include:

- **Does it say what I want to say?**
- **Is it in the right order?**
- **Is the form right?**

Many teachers offer their children sets of questions to get them started on revision, such as:

- **Does everything make sense?**
- **Could I add something?**
- **Should I leave anything out?**
- **Are there any parts in the wrong order?**

You might display these questions as posters or cards and children might use them independently, or with a friend. They may be the first step towards enabling children to look critically at their work without the prompting of the teacher.

Revision may involve minor adjustments, like insertions, crossings out, etc., or it may necessitate rewriting and moving blocks. Some of these strategies are more difficult than others and it is likely that children will need a great deal of support before they are able to use them independently. There are particular techniques to which they can be introduced, such as the use of scissors to physically cut out sections to resequence writing. They may also be fairly resistant to alterations which involve crossing out sections of writing (perhaps because crossings out are often associated in children's minds with mistakes), and will need special reassurance that this kind of revision is approved of by their teachers.

Revising one's own writing can be quite difficult, even for adults. Writers are often too close to their own writing to be able to look at it with a properly critical eye. Because of this, it can often be useful to encourage children to work in small groups to help revise each other's writing. Fresh eyes can spot problems and also help the writer become more able to see them.

EDITING

When the writing is at a stage where the author is starting to think about a final draft then editing becomes necessary. Editing involves correcting the surface features of the text: spelling, grammar, punctuation, etc. Most children are familiar with this in the form of a teacher's 'marking'. Some teachers mark these surface features automatically, and so children set great store by them. This at least means that editing is the easiest part of the process to introduce. These features of language are important, and although you can correct them quickly and accurately, it is preferable for children to correct work themselves. This is not only a step towards independence, it also allows children to develop transferable strategies for future work.

To support the children in doing this you might use wallcharts and cards offering questions and advice. Such wallcharts may even introduce children to professional proof-readers' codes and children usually enjoy using these. These charts can be used by individuals, or more often, pairs of children. Peer editing is helpful in that it offers the child support, advice and opinions, which can be accepted or rejected depending on the author's judgement. It is also allows realistic organisation of your time as purposeful, task-oriented discussion can take place without you being present.

PUBLICATION AND EVALUATION

Drafting is a very powerful process that allows children to concentrate on the various elements of writing separately. The emphasis is on producing a better quality product for an audience. This means, of course, that children need to publish and evaluate their writing. In this context publish means simply 'to make public', and this can take many forms. Some work may be read out to a teacher, friend, group or class, perhaps in a designated 'sharing time'. Publication could also mean displaying work so that it becomes reading material in a real sense, from a single piece of writing on the wall to a book written for younger children by a group. In all cases it is important that publication should have the appropriate form and that final decisions about content and so on should be made by the author. When the publication reaches its intended audience then any sort of response can be used for evaluation. This may be between you and the child, among a small group, or more publicly. In any case both you and the children need to understand the need for constructive criticism.

When publication is the perceived end-point of the writing children are helped to develop their awareness of audience. This has an effect upon both the composition and transcription processes which children need to begin to take account of early in their writing experience. They need, in general, to have experience of writing for a range of purposes.

Planning for the process

The process of writing that we have just explored is not linear in operation in the sense of a series of steps through which writers proceed in order. Rather, the process is recursive and reflective with several parts operating simultaneously.

This has several implications for the teaching of writing which you might consider. You need to allow for these things in organising your teaching of writing.

- **Children need time to reflect on their writing.**
- **Allowance needs to be given for the erratic nature of the process.**
- **Children might benefit from discussing their approaches to writing with their classmates.**

Teaching the writing process

There are a number of teaching strategies you might employ, both in and out of the literacy hour, to teach writing to Key Stage 2 children. Some of these are described in this section, with some examples of how they might be employed.

Shared reading

No, you are not reading the wrong chapter! Shared reading is an essential step in the effective teaching of writing. In the course of reading a shared text with a class, you can, as well as focusing on teaching them how to read this text, also teach a good deal about how the text is structured. A highly developed familiarity with the structure of a text is necessary if they are subsequently to write texts like this themselves. Put crudely, you would not expect children to write very good poetry if they had never read any or had any read to them. The same is true of all text types. As an example, look at the following transcription of some writing produced by a seven-year-old who was asked to write a set of instructions for how to plant cress seeds.

Cress

> We had some seeds and Mrs Lewis gave us some seeds in our hands then we sprinkled the seed on the plate. Then Mrs Lewis gave us a piece of paper to cover the seeds. We are going to leave them to grow. Every day we will check the seeds to see if they have grown.

This may be a fairly accurate account of what happened in the lesson, but it is not a set of instructions; it lacks basic features such as a statement of the goal ('How to plant cress seeds'), a list of materials and equipment needed, a sequence of steps to follow and the correct use of tense (the imperative would be more appropriate than simple past tense).

You can draw children's attention to these features by using texts such as instructions in shared reading sessions. The following is an example of how you might do this using an instructional text.

Classroom story

Miss R's Year 5 class was beginning some work on writing instructional texts. In a shared reading session, she introduced them to the recipe for making pizza shown in Figure 9.1. After reading the text together they discussed the following points:

- *How do you know this is a recipe?* **(It tells you how to cook something. There's a list of ingredients.)**
- *What kind of text is that?* **(It tells you how to do something. Instructions.)**
- *Can you think of any other texts that are like recipes and tell you how to do something?* **(Rules for playing games. Instructions for fixing the computer.)**
- *What does a recipe always begin with?* **(There will always be a title. The title tells you what you are going to make.)**
- *What does the first part of this recipe tell you?* **(How big a pizza it will make. How long it takes.)**
- *What does the next part tell you?* **(The ingredients. What you need to make the pizza.)**
- *How are the ingredients organised?* **(A list. Measurements for each item.)**
- *What follows the ingredients?* **(What you have to do. The method.)**
- *What do you notice about these directions?* **(They are in the form of a numbered list. They use commands, or imperatives. They refer to time, either directly or by the use of chronological connectives, until, then, etc.)**

Making Pizza	
This recipe will make a 12 to 16 inch pizza Preparation time: 15 minutes Cooking time: 20 minutes	
Ingredients	**Directions**
1 cup warm water 1 tablespoon white sugar 2¼ teaspoons active dried yeast 3 tablespoons olive oil 1 teaspoon salt 2½ cups plain flour	1. Stir the sugar and yeast into the water until they are dissolved. 2. Add the olive oil and the salt and then stir. 3. Stir in the flour until it is well blended. 4. Let the dough rest for 10 minutes. 5. Dip your fingers in olive oil and pat the dough into a flat pan or onto a pizza stone. 6. If you wish, you can sprinkle basil, thyme or other seasonings on top. 7. Place your favourite pizza toppings on top. Use tomato paste and cheese as a base. 8. Bake for 15 to 20 minutes in a preheated oven at 200°C.

Figure 9.1 A recipe for making pizza

Through this shared reading, you can both familiarise your children with the key structural features of the text type they will be going on to write and focus their attention on crucial linguistic and grammatical features. This knowledge will later be applied when they come to write their own texts.

You might also want to involve your children in compiling a checklist of these crucial text type features. This is a learning activity in its own right as they now have to think abstractly about text features. It can also be used later as an aide-memoire when they come to write. Miss R went on to do this with her Year 5 class. The questions she used to prompt them, together with some of their answers, are presented in Figure 9.2.

Thinking about recipes		
Questions the children were asked	**Things you might point out**	**Some of the children's responses**
What comes first in a recipe?	*The title of the dish. The goal of the recipe.*	What you're going to make. The name of what you're making.
What comes next?	*List of ingredients.*	What you need. All your equipment and things.
How are these laid out on the page?	*Vertical lists.*	Lists.
In what order are the ingredients listed?	*This is debatable.*	The order in which you use them. The biggest things first.
What comes next in the recipe?	*Directions for making the dish.*	What you have to do.
In what order are these listed?	*Chronological.*	The right order.
Why?	*Because that's how you use them.*	You'd get mixed up.
How are they laid out on the page?	*Usually a numbered list.*	Number of steps. 1, 2, 3, 4...
What tense are they written in?	*Imperative*	Do this...
Do they use passive or active verbs?	*Active.*	You have to do actions.
Who is the audience for a recipe?	*There is an implied second person – an implied but not stated 'you'.*	Anyone making the dish. The cook.
What style of language would you expect?	*Unembellished, businesslike, formal.*	Plain and simple.
Why?	*Ease of use – you need instant reference.*	It has to be quick to read.

Figure 9.2 Key features of recipes

Shared writing

As well as ensuring that your children understand the key features of what they are going to write, you need to show them how to compose and transcribe texts like this. Teacher demonstrations of this kind are crucial teaching opportunities for two main reasons:

1. They can draw children's attention to many of the invisible elements of a writer's craft, such as the thought processes which underpin the production of the writing.
2. They can show the children that you are a writer too, not just someone who tells them to write.

Shared writing is a powerful teaching strategy and involves much more than just writing down what children say, acting as competent secretary to their authors. Shared writing provides you with opportunities to:

- **work with the whole class, to model, explore and discuss the decisions that writers make when they are writing;**
- **make links between reading and writing explicit:**
- **demonstrate how writers use language to achieve particular effects;**
- **remove temporarily some of the problems of orchestrating writing skills by taking on the burden of some aspects, for example, spelling and handwriting, thereby enabling the children to focus exclusively on how composition works;**
- **focus on particular aspects of the writing process, such as planning, composing, revising or editing;**
- **scaffold children in the use of appropriate technical language to discuss what writers do and think.**

While you are doing a shared writing activity, you will need to think about some of the following aspects.

- **Discuss with the children the audience and purpose of the writing task you are engaged in, and discuss how that will influence the content, structure and grammar of what is written.**
- **Rehearse sentences orally before you write them down. This offers an excellent model for children's own composition as it encourages thoughtfulness.**
- **Emphasise your use of punctuation, and verbalise your reasons for using particular marks.**
- **Reread what you have written at regular intervals. This encourages children to think about the flow from one sentence to another.**
- **Hold debates with yourself as you decide between possible options in your writing. Verbalise the ways you decide what works best.**
- **You might want to make the occasional deliberate mistake in your writing. This will help keep the children's attention and will also allow you deliberately to focus on particular common errors.**

Of course, not every shared writing session need be the same and there are three main teaching techniques you can use to help children gradually move towards independence.

MODELLING WRITING

You will need to demonstrate how to write a text and while doing this you should think aloud, modelling the thought processes you use while writing. You might do such things as the following.

- **Rehearse a sentence orally before writing it, make changes to it, explaining why you chose certain words and not others, point out mistakes you have made or points on which you can improve.**
- **Show them what you do in writing when you run out of ideas (reread what you have written, discuss it with another person, brainstorm some ideas, refer back to your plan).**
- **Show them what you do when you need to write quickly (write in note form, use abbreviations).**
- **Show what you do when you don't know how a word is spelt (try it several ways to see what looks right, write what you think and mark it to check later, use a similarly meaning word that you can spell!).**

SCRIBING

Here you invite the children to take part in the composition process, while you transcribe an agreed version of what they say. You might:

- **Ask them to suggest a sentence at a time, which you respond to, expanding and modifying as you feel, but explaining why you are doing this.**
- **Take two or more suggestions and ask the class to give you reasons for preferring one or the other.**
- **Give them time to compose in writing, perhaps using jotter books, or small whiteboards, before asking for their suggestions.**

PROMPTED WRITING

Here you ask the children to write short sections with very clear guidelines from you. This will allow time for children to practise particular points in their writing. You might:

- **ask them for a sentence that tells you one more thing about the main character in the story you are writing;**
- **ask for two more sentences, each containing at least one subordinate clause;**
- **ask them to write the next persuasive point in the argument you have already planned.**

Guided writing

Guided writing is an additional supported step towards independent writing. Children can be offered clear support but the onus is on them to make decisions, compose and revise their own texts. There are three main purposes for guided writing.

1. *To help children plan and draft their independent work.* You can support this work by helping children to orchestrate all the decisions needed to draft their own text. This might involve children in such things as:

   - **retelling a story they have previously had read to them, where the content is predetermined and their task is to find a way of communicating that content;**

- writing an explanatory paragraph following a model they have earlier discussed in shared reading;
- using the computer to rewrite a piece of formal or archaic writing to make it more conversational or modern.

2. *To help children revise and edit work already begun*. Encourage them to share their writing with the group and:

- reread it to check its clarity;
- enhance the vocabulary choices they have made by responding to suggestions from other children;
- work on strengthening particular words, phrases or text sections such as introductions and endings;
- check their use of cohesion, such as consistent use of pronouns, use of connectives and consistency of tense.

3. *To provide differentiated support for particular children or groups*. Children will need greater levels of individual teaching than will be possible in whole class work and you can use guided writing to:

- repeat a shared writing session with more support for the less confident writers;
- prepare certain children for a forthcoming shared writing session by previewing the key ideas they will be using;
- stretch more able writers in composing or editing activities;
- work intensively with less able writers.

Scaffolding writing

Some children will learn most of what they need to know about writing a particular text type from their shared reading and writing sessions. For many, however, the jump from being shown how to write in a particular way to being able to write that way independently is simply too big for them to make easily. They need more support as they begin to learn to be independent writers.

This phase involves scaffolded writing, during which you can offer children strategies to aid their writing, which they can use without an adult necessarily being alongside them. One popular such strategy is the use of writing frames, which were earlier described as an aid to planning writing. They can also act both as a way of increasing a child's experience of a particular type of writing and as a substitute for the teacher's direct interventions which encourage children to extend their writing.

A writing frame consists of a skeleton outline to scaffold children's writing of a particular text type. The skeleton framework consists of different key words or phrases, according to the particular generic form. The template of starters, connectives and sentence modifiers which constitute a writing frame gives children a structure within which they can concentrate on communicating what they want to say, rather than getting lost in the form. However, by using the form, children become increasingly familiar with it.

Some example writing frames were given earlier in the chapter; further photocopiable examples can be found in Lewis and Wray (1997 and 1998).

Notice how writing with this kind of frame scaffolds writing in a number of ways:

- **It does not present writers with a blank page. There is comfort in the fact that there is already some writing on this page. This alone can be enough to encourage weaker writers to write at greater length.**
- **The frame provides a series of prompts to children's writing. Using the frame is rather like having a dialogue with the page and the prompts serve to model the register of that particular piece of writing.**
- **The frame deliberately includes connectives beyond the simple 'and then'. Extended use of frames can result in children spontaneously using these more elaborate connectives in other writing.**
- **The frame is designed around the typical structure of a particular genre. It thus gives children access to this structure and implicitly teaches them a way of writing this type of text.**

You should always begin your use of a frame with shared writing, discussion and teacher modelling before moving on to collaborative writing (teacher and children together) and then to the child undertaking writing supported by the frame. This oral, teacher modelling, joint construction pattern of teaching is vital, for it not only models the generic form and teaches the words that signal connections and transitions, but it also provides opportunities for developing children's oral language and their thinking. Some children, especially those with learning difficulties, may need many oral sessions and sessions in which their teacher acts as a scribe before they are ready to attempt their own writing.

You would find it useful to make 'big' versions of the frames for use in shared writing. It is important that the children understand that the frame is a supportive draft and words may be crossed out or substituted. Extra sentences may be added or surplus starters crossed out. The frame should be treated as a flexible aid, not a rigid form.

When the children have a purpose for writing you may decide to offer them a frame:

- **when they first attempt independent writing in an unfamiliar text type and a scaffold might be helpful to them;**
- **when a child/group of children appear stuck in a particular mode of writing, e.g. constantly using 'and then' … 'and then' when writing an account;**
- **when they 'wander' between text types in a way that demonstrates a lack of understanding of a particular type, e.g. while writing an instructional text such as a recipe they start in the second person ('First you beat the egg') but then shift into a recount ('Next I stirred in the flour');**
- **when they have written something in one structure (often a personal recount) which would be more appropriate in a different form, e.g. writing up a science experiment as a personal recount.**

Writing frames can be helpful to children of all ages and all abilities. You might, however, find them particularly useful with children of average writing ability and with those who find writing difficult. It would of course be unnecessary to use the frame with writers already confident and fluent in a particular text type but they can be used to introduce such writers to new types. The aim with all children is for them to reach the stage of assimilating the generic structures and language features into their independent writing repertoires. Children therefore need to use the frames less and less as their knowledge of a particular form increases. At this later stage, when children begin to show evidence of independent usage, you may need only to have a master copy of the frames available as help cards for those occasions when children need a prompt. A box of such help cards could be a part of the writing area in which children are encouraged to refer to many different aids to their writing. This is one way of encouraging children to begin to make independent decisions about their own learning.

Also, as children become familiar with the frame structures, there are a number of alternative support structures which can be used, such as prompt sheets containing lists of possible ways of connecting ideas together. A number of these will be found in Lewis and Wray (1998).

Teaching writing at Key Stage 2 :

a summary of key points

- **The process of writing needs to be taught directly.**
- **The process involves elements such as planning, composition, transcription, revision, editing and publication.**
- **Teaching the writing of a particular text type begins with familiarising children with the features of this text type, through shared reading and a progressive focus on key features.**
- **Shared writing, during which the teacher models how to compose a particular text, is a vital teaching strategy.**
- **Guided writing gradually puts the onus more and more onto the children in writing.**
- **Many children will need their writing to be scaffolded, perhaps by the use of writing frames.**

Further reading

Lewis, M. and Wray, D. (1994) *Developing Children's Non-fiction Writing*. Leamington Spa: Scholastic.

Professional Standards for QTS

→ **3.3.2b, 3.3.3**

Section 3 of the Professional Standards for Qualified Teacher Status includes a new emphasis on teaching the performing arts as well as English at Key Stage 1 or 2. This enables useful links to be made for the teaching of speaking and listening with drama, art and music, as well as cross-curricular approaches including history, geography and other foundation subjects. You are also required to teach clearly structured lessons or sequences of work and employ interactive teaching methods and collaborative group work (especially relevant to the teaching of speaking and listening).

The Handbook accompanying the Standards clarifies these requirements and you will find it helpful to read through the appropriate section of this Handbook for further support.

Curriculum Guidance for the Foundation Stage/National Curriculum programmes of study

The Early Learning Goals suggest that, by the end of the Foundation Stage, most children should be able to:

- enjoy listening to and using spoken and written language, and readily turn to it in their play and learning;
- explore and experiment with sounds, words and texts;
- listen with enjoyment and respond to stories, songs and other music, rhymes and poems and make up their own stories, songs, rhymes and poems;
- use language to imagine and recreate roles and experiences;
- use talk to organise, sequence and clarify thinking, ideas, feelings and events;
- sustain attentive listening, responding to what they have heard by relevant comments, questions or actions;
- interact with others, negotiating plans and activities and taking turns in conversation;
- extend their vocabulary, exploring the meanings and sounds of new words;
- retell narratives in the correct sequence, drawing on the language patterns of stories;
- speak clearly and audibly with confidence and control and show awareness of the listener, for example by their use of conventions such as greetings, 'please' and 'thank you'.

The National Curriculum for English requirements are that, at Key Stage I, pupils should be taught the importance of language that is clear, fluent and interesting. They should be encouraged to speak with confidence, making themselves clear through organising what they say and choosing words with precision. They should also be encouraged to listen with growing attention and concentration, to respond appropriately and effectively to what they have heard, and to ask and answer questions that clarify their understanding and indicate thoughtfulness about the matter under discussion.

At Key Stage 2 they should be taught to use vocabulary and syntax that enables the communication of more complex meanings. In discussions, they should be given opportunities to make a range of contributions, including making exploratory and tentative comments when ideas are being collected together, and making reasoned, evaluative comments as the discussion moves to conclusions or action. Pupils should be taught to evaluate their own talk and reflect on how it varies. They should also be taught to listen carefully, and to recall and re-present important features of an argument, talk, presentation, reading, radio or television programme and to qualify or justify what they think after listening to other opinions or accounts.

The National Literacy Strategy

The National Literacy Strategy focuses deliberately on literacy, yet makes it clear that all this work needs to go hand in hand with, and is to a degree dependent on, the development of speaking and listening. This is explained in greater detail below.

Introduction

Talk is central to the primary curriculum and particularly important in English. Encouraging children to listen carefully and become confident speakers in a wide range of different contexts will provide them with a strong foundation for communication in the broadest sense, as well as establishing a framework for the teaching of reading and writing. The ability to communicate clearly and directly in standard English underpins all effective teaching, so it is vital that beginning teachers learn to develop a clear speaking voice.

The chapter starts by setting out the statutory requirements for oral work in the National Curriculum and National Literacy Strategy (NLS), before moving on to some detailed ideas for developing effective talk in the classroom from the early years onwards. Many of the activities draw on drama techniques. Above all, well-planned oral work in the classroom can be enjoyable, interesting and imaginative, and can extend pupils' experience and understanding in a number of ways.

Oral work in the National Curriculum and National Literacy Strategy

Speaking and listening are essential foundations for literacy development, and

effective teaching of literacy will offer opportunities to promote oral skills.
(National Literacy Strategy Framework for Teaching, 1998, p. 94)

The importance of speaking and listening is underlined by its position as the first attainment target (ATI) in the English National Curriculum (DfEE/QCA, 1999). A wide range of oral activities, including discussion work and drama, are included in the Programmes of Study at Key Stages 1 and 2 (KS1 and 2). The aim of these is to develop a variety of oral skills such as storytelling, turn-taking, discussing, explaining and persuading, as well as listening skills such as concentrating, responding and recalling.

The National Literacy Strategy also stresses the importance of 'high quality oral work' (p. 8) in effective and successful teaching of the literacy hour, characterised by 'discursive' and 'interactive' (p. 8) strategies such as questioning, modelling and investigating. These are seen as underpinning many of the NLS objectives and are designed to encourage and extend pupils' own oral skills. The NLS *Framework for Teaching* does not explicitly state how and when such strategies can be used, and initial use of the *Framework* led in some cases to over-didactic teaching with insufficient oral contributions by pupils, particularly during shared reading. However, if you look closely at the content specified in the *Framework*, many activities, such as storytelling (NLS Reception and Year 1), writing and reciting poetry, riddles and tongue twisters (NLS Year 2), inevitably involve oral strategies. In addition, the more recent additional activities (NLS, 1999) include explicit recommendations for promoting more interactive work in the literacy hour, such as simple drama activities.

Encouraging talk in the early years

It is not always realised how much talking young children do at home, for instance while playing on their own or with each other, and with adults at mealtimes, bath-time and bedtime.

RESEARCH SUMMARY

Gordon Wells' research in the 1980s showed that young children talked far more at home than at school, and that talk at home was often child-led whereas talk at school was more likely to be teacher-led (see Wells, 1987).

While it is clearly important that children learn how to operate in different situations, it is also important for teachers to realise the effects that their own language may have on young children's language development.

There is no shortage of activities to do in nursery and reception classes which start from and extend young children's early language skills, as well as helping with early number and science work.

Rhymes

Children love rhymes of all kinds. As well as being fun, rhymes help to increase vocabulary and children's early reading and writing skills through developing phonemic awareness (see Chapter 5). There are many kinds of rhymes, the most common being nursery rhymes; there are also action, nonsense, finger and number rhymes which help children to develop rhythm and simple coordination as well as counting skills. The frequent repetition and use of refrains help to reinforce the vocabulary and rhymes, and young children enjoy being able to learn and recite the rhymes by heart (NLS Reception year, text level 10). Plenty of rhymes can be found in *This Little Puffin*, the Opies' collection of children's playground games and rhymes (1984), or *Inky Pinky Ponky* (Rosen and Steele, 1990). A simple example of an action rhyme is shown below, with actions in brackets:

Five little peas in a pea pod pressed.	(clench fist to represent pod)
First one grew, then another,	(hold up one then two fingers)
and so did all the rest.	(hold up other fingers in turn)
They grew and they grew	(move both hands away from
and they didn't stop,	each other as the pod grows)
until one day the pod went POP!	(clap hands to make a loud pop)

Rhymes like this are ideally spoken or sung in the carpeted area, with enough space for the children to make simple movements. For rhymes which demand more space (e.g. 'five little speckled frogs' in which some children can be frogs in the pond), the children could sit in a circle.

Sensory play

Sensory play means play with sand and water, or with other materials such as clay, play-dough etc. The children will usually talk among themselves about what they are doing and what the water or sand feels like. If the teacher or classroom assistant 'plays' along-side the children, plenty of opportunities for extended talking and questioning arise. For example, if a child is filling a bucket with water, you might say, 'Now try pouring the water on to the water wheel. What happens when you do that?' Simple vocabulary about capacity and weight such as 'full', empty', 'heavy' and 'light' can be introduced (NLS Reception year, word level 10–11). The children can be encouraged to describe how the sand or water feels as they play with it. Introduce plenty of different-sized containers for comparison.

Here are some ideas for sensory activities for small groups:

- **'feely' bags with differently shaped objects (e.g. ball, cube, ring) – ask the children to describe the shapes;**
- **'feely' bags with contrasting materials (e.g. satin and hessian, wood and metal) to introduce vocabulary like 'smooth' and 'rough';**
- **containers with foods of different textures (e.g. jelly, jam, peeled orange, hard boiled egg) to encourage descriptive responses;**
- **blindfold tasting to experience different flavours such as sweet and sour (e.g. apple juice, lemon juice).**

The last two activities need careful planning and organisation to avoid possible mess (aprons and paper towels need to be on hand), and clear controls need to be estab-lished to avoid over-excitement. You also need to check any possible allergies or dietary habits if food tasting is involved. In spite of these caveats, these are rewarding activities that often encourage the shyest pupil to open up and talk.

Imaginative play

Imaginative play is a particularly effective way to encourage young children to talk. However, it will not happen by itself. Imaginative play needs careful organisation and thought, with sensitive teacher intervention in order to extend the children's language development. Nursery and reception classes often have home corners for domestic play, but if left unattended this can lead to stereotyped play with limited gender roles. A more effective alternative is to set up varied role-play areas, which can be developed with the involvement of the children themselves, and should be changed regularly.

Classroom story

Books can be a useful starting point for role-play areas, which can also be related to topic work. For example, a topic on food in a reception class involved reading Mrs Wobble the Waitress (Ahlberg), *and led to planning and making a café area in the classroom. The children discussed what they wanted In the café, planned and designed the menus and signs (NLS Reception year, text level 15) and took on the roles of cook, waiter and waitress, receptionist and customers. As a culmination of the project, the children invited their parents into the café, and served them fruit drinks and cakes, which they had made themselves. In this case, the role-play developed from an activity for small groups into a more public event with a real purpose and audience.*

Other role-play areas which have been used successfully include real life situations such as a doctor's surgery, hospital, optician, travel agent, shop (e.g. bakers, greengrocers, clothes shop, newsagent), or imaginary/fairy story places, such as the three bears' house, gingerbread cottage, the yellow submarine, an underwater kingdom. The teacher can easily and naturally take on a role in these situations and enter into the role-play as and when it seems appropriate. However, it is important to be sensitive to the children's space and either wait to be invited or ask if you can join in.

Some other useful hints are listed below.

- **Restrict numbers in the role-play area to three or four at a time. Keep a record of who has used it so that everyone can take a turn.**
- **Make role cards or labels for the different roles (e.g. doctor, nurse, patient) for easy identification and to ensure the children swap roles regularly. This helps to avoid gender stereotyping of roles and to alter power relations (e.g. to avoid the same child always being in charge).**
- **Introduce an event or challenge into the role-play in order to maintain motivation and interest (e.g. the shoe shop has a sale; the three bears hold a party).**

These activities need much careful organisation and planning. However, at least some of the work can be built into the literacy hour (e.g. stories as a starting point in shared reading; making notices in guided writing). Time in the area itself can also be one of the activities during group work or built into other times of the day as there may well be cross-curricular links (e.g. travel agent links to geography; optician links to science).

Storytelling and traditional stories

The use of traditional stories, storytelling and retelling have long been in the repertoire of experienced early years teachers (Grainger, 1997). More recently, storytelling has been placed as a central activity in the early years National Literacy Framework (NLS Reception year, text level 4–8) as well as the National Curriculum English at Key Stage I.

You need to introduce a wide range of stories to the children, both in picture book format and through oral telling. This is a good opportunity to include traditional stories and folk tales from all around the world (e.g. Anansi stories from the Caribbean, Russian Baba Yaga stories) in order to broaden horizons from Hans Andersen and Grimm, and avoid race, gender and class stereotypes. Many children will only be familiar with traditional stories from Walt Disney film versions; returning to the originals will broaden their experience. Many stories are now available on tape for quiet listening, but nothing equals the power of the direct approach. Look out for local storytellers who will visit the school, or theatre-in-education companies who can bring stories to life in a vivid and immediate way.

In retelling stories in an interactive way, teachers can begin to reinforce traditional story openings ('once upon a time') and endings, as well as story structure and narrative. This helps children when they are learning to read, as well as in writing their own stories later. Children's confidence can be developed through storytelling activities, as well as early cooperative skills. Using and telling stories in different languages can help bilingual children and those with English as an additional language to develop their new language as well as reinforcing skills in their first language.

Classroom story

Most children already know the story of Goldilocks and the three bears but it has plenty of potential for development and oral work. In a nursery class, the teacher told the story to the children and then asked them to retell it with her. They drew pictures of their favourite part of the story. They made porridge, added different flavours (salt, sugar, honey, etc.) and talked about which they preferred. With the teacher's help they turned the home corner into the three bears' cottage and re-enacted the story through role-play. They read and discussed Goldilocks' letter of apology to the three bears in The Jolly Postman *(Ahlberg). A parent helper dressed up as Baby Bear and appeared in the classroom lost and upset because her chair had been broken by Goldilocks. The children helped her by asking if she knew the way home, suggested phoning home or the police, and took her to the school office to make the call. This led to further discussion with the teacher about times they had been lost or upset (DfEE, Early Learning Goals, 1999).*

Puppets

Puppets are another valuable resource in the early years classroom, and can help oral work, storymaking and manual dexterity. Simple finger puppets made from felt can be easily made with young children and shoeboxes can be transformed into puppet theatres. Many glove puppets, usually of animals, are also available commercially, and can be used effectively by the teacher and children alike (see the NLS Progression in Phonics video of a puppet being used to teach phonemes in the literacy hour). Often children who have been reluctant to speak will talk through their puppets: it is a less immediate, and therefore sometimes less threatening, means of encouraging talk than role-play. Many of the features of storytelling mentioned above can also be incorporated in work with puppets. Using puppets also helps to develop an early sense of audience and performance, and encourages cooperation and interaction with others (see DfEE, Early Learning Goals, 1999).

Speaking and listening at Key Stage 1

Many of the ideas and strategies for oral work already introduced can be adapted and developed further at Key Stage 1. The English National Curriculum emphasises group discussions and drama, and the development of imaginative responses as well as concentration and confidence in speaking (NC English, 1999, KS1 Speaking and Listening). The new Professional Standards for QTS emphasise interactive strategies and the performaing arts (3.3.2b and 3.3.3).

Responding to texts

There are numerous possibilities at Key Stage 1 to develop oral responses to picture books, poems and rhymes, building on work already done in the nursery and reception classes. An extension of rhyming activities in the early years leads into action stories and the beginnings of movement and drama (NC English KS1 Reading 6e; NLS Year 1, Term 1, text level 6). A particularly effective example is *We're Going on a Bear Hunt* (Rosen and Oxenbury), which can be carried out sitting on the carpet or enacted in a larger space with the children moving around the room. The beginning of the story, with suggested actions for the carpeted area, is shown below, with capitals for spoken emphasis and actions in brackets.

	(start rhythm by slapping knees: 1-2 1-2)
We're going on a bear hunt.	(continue rhythm to show walking)
We're going to catch a BIG one.	(emphasise 'big' with hands far apart)
It's a BEAUTIFUL day.	(hands make circle to show sun)
I'm not scared.	(shake head for extra emphasis)
Uh-oh! Grass! Long wavy grass.	(hands up and down to show grass)

Refrain:

We can't go OVER it	(lift hands to show 'over')
We can't go UNDER it	(lower hands to show 'under')
We can't go ROUND it	(move hands round)
We'll have to go THROUGH it.	(move hands forward or 'through')
Swishy-swashy, swishy-swashy	(move hands from side to side)

The action builds up with a succession of obstacles which the children have to over-come (useful for introducing prepositions of place). The refrain is repeated at each obstacle, with a different sound and action, and the adventure ends with a quick retreat home with the actions in reverse order when a large bear is finally found. It is great fun, and children in Key Stage I enjoy this kind of activity as much as those in the early years. For Year I children, you will need to build up to this after practice with simpler action rhymes, and accompanying stories with actions or sounds. Associated activities include hearing and making up riddles, tongue twisters and non-sense rhymes, which develop and extend children's phonemic awareness in enjoyable ways (NLS Y2 Term 3, text level 11).

Role-play and role-play areas can also provide enriching language experiences at Key Stage I (NC English KSI S and L IIa; NLS YI, Term I, text level 7 and I6), and are particu-larly effective with stories as a stimulus.

Classroom story

Post office role-play
A topic on communication in a Year 1 class was sparked off by reading Janet and Allan Ahlberg's The Jolly Postman and led to the setting up of a post office in the activity area outside the classroom. The teacher arranged for a parent who was a postman to talk to the children about his job. They also visited the local post office to see what they would need to include. After this preparation, the children made a large post box, designed and made forms and wrote out notices (NLS Year 1, Term 1, text level 16). They took turns to serve in the post office and be customers. The teacher also set aside a writing corner in the classroom and encouraged the children to write letters to her or each other, which they posted in the post box. Although the children's writing was at an early stage, the motivation which was generated by the project led many children to make dramatic improvements in their ability to write simple sentences as well as in their oral work (NC English KS1 Writing 11 and 12).

Storytelling can also be extended at Key Stage I, and can be linked to simple drama techniques (NC English KSI, S and L 4 and II; NLS YI, Term I, text level 3; Term 2, text level 4, 5 and 9; Term 3, text level 3, 5 and 6). The example below uses the traditional story of Goldilocks and the three bears again, but shows how it can be extended in dif-ferent ways at Key Stage I.

Classroom story

The teacher of a Year 1 class started with an indirect way into the story by taking on the role of Goldilocks' mother. She enacted a short breakfast time scene where she discovered Goldilocks was missing ('Goldilocks! Your porridge is getting cold') and then enlisted the children's help to find her. This involved recounting the main events of the story, drawing a map showing the route from Goldilock's house to the three bears' cottage in the woods, a police investigation including 'hot seating' where the three bears were interviewed about their reactions to events, and a 'freeze frame' where groups of children made tableaux or still photographs of the main events for the local newspaper. They also discussed and wrote news flashes for radio or television and short accounts for the newspaper (NC English, KS1 Writing, 1, 2, 9–12). ICT was involved in tape recording the interviews and word processing the news items (Professional Standards for QTS 3.3.10). Finally, Goldilocks was tracked down and interviewed or hot seated to find out what had made her run away to the woods.

There are many other ways of developing oral work in response to texts at Key Stage I. Aidan Chambers (1993) suggests some ways in to discussion, through his 'tell me' techniques, which he argues are more direct and concrete than the often off-putting question 'why?' Through the 'tell me' approach, children are encouraged to talk about what they first noticed about a book or story, what they liked and disliked, and to point out any puzzles and patterns. This can lead into detailed work on a story in order to share ideas, and find clues and evidence to support a particular view. The techniques are very useful in promoting high quality group discussion work, and can also lead into writing through the keeping of reading journals. Although Chambers' work predates the literacy hour, the suggested activities can easily be adapted to fit shared and particularly guided reading sessions.

Story-making and talking about writing

As in the early years' work, many of the oral activities about books and poems described above, especially storytelling and drama, link to children's own writing at Key Stage I (see NC English 1999, KSI Writing). As well as discussing story structures, characters and actions in relation to texts, children can be encouraged to create their own stories orally in readiness for writing.

A story circle is an enjoyable way into story-making, and also enhances imagination, listening skills and turn taking (NC English, KSI S and L 2, 3, 8 and 10; NLS Y2, Term I, text level 3 and 4). It is best carried out in groups rather than with the whole class, and can be fitted easily into a group activity in the literacy hour. Building on games like 'I went to market and I bought a...' which are essentially listing and memory exercises, story circles can involve more complex sequencing of ideas and events. For example, the teacher or a pupil can start a story with a simple opening, for example 'One morning Sally went to see her friend Joe'. The story is passed round the circle, with each person starting their contribution with 'fortunately' or 'unfortunately', which can give rise to highly amusing results. An alternative is to use different words and phrases to link each person's turn, such as 'then', 'suddenly', 'meanwhile', 'after that', trying not to repeat the same ones (NLS Y2, Term I, sentence level 2, text level II).

Another variation is to place one or more objects (e.g. a hat, a ring, a box) in the centre of the circle: the group has to make up a short story in which the objects play an important part. A discussion about the objects, considering such factors as whom they belong to, what use or importance they have and where they were found, needs to precede the story itself. Once the ingredients are clear, then the group can begin to construct the story. The teacher can introduce a particular focus, such as what the characters are like, who owns the objects, or what actions led to the finding of the objects.

Classroom story

After reading Michael Morpurgo's Wreck of the Zanzibar *to a Year 2 class, the teacher started a group story circle by showing them a bottle she had supposedly found washed up on the beach. It contained a message which was very old and torn, but which was partly legible and was from Richard Jenkins, who had been shipwrecked on a desert island and was asking for help. The group were asked to discuss who they thought Richard Jenkins was, when he lived (there was no date on the message) and why/how/by whom he might have been shipwrecked. They had to use the clues in the message and to list all their ideas and unanswered questions on a large sheet of paper. The next day, with the teacher's help to review their work, they decided on the beginning of their story and built up the events and character profiles using the evidence and ideas they had gathered the previous day. At the teacher's suggestion, they 'hot seated' two of the group who took on the roles of Richard's best friend and his sister. At this point one of the group acted as scribe to start writing down the story which was completed in extended writing time, word processed and illustrated with maps of the island to form a class book (NC English KS1 S and L 3, Writing 2 and 9; NLS Y2, Term 2, text level 14; Term 3 text level 10).*

Other useful starting points for story-making are photographs. They can be collected from magazines and newspapers, but this may limit the images to film and pop stars or people in news stories, which can predetermine the direction of the children's ideas. It is better to use specially prepared collections – for example, photographs of families, in which a range of people are presented, and there are accompanying guidelines for teachers. Discussions of photographs need to be handled sensitively in order to avoid reinforcing prejudices, for instance when looking at a family of travellers, but with careful intervention photos can broaden children's horizons and viewpoints and help to challenge gender, race and class stereotypes.

Classroom story

An able Year 2 class had been discussing families following a reading of Judy Blume's Superfudge. *The teacher used a family photopack to consider a range of family units before moving into some dramatic writing. First she put up a selection of the photographs around the walls, asked the children to look carefully at them and put an initial beside the ones they liked best. Then she grouped them according to their choices, and gave each group one photograph. The photos were mounted on a large sheet of paper and the groups were asked to write down as many questions as they could think of, with arrows to the people concerned (e.g. 'Why is he wearing that funny hat?' 'Why does she look so upset?') and then to fill in speech or thought bubbles which helped to explain or answer their questions (e.g. 'This hat hurts but I wanted to look smart'. 'My brother just hit me because I took his Mars bar'). With the teacher's help, the children discussed the family relationships and related them to their own experiences where they could. The next stage was to tape record these phrases and then add some dialogue between the family members. The children eventually presented their tape recordings to each other (NC English, KS1 S and L 3,4, 10 and 11; NLS Y2, Term 2, text level 14; Y3, Term 1, text level 14).*

Tape recorders can be useful tools for recording story ideas, especially when children find writing difficult, and can be used to redraft and edit different versions of stories. They are also effective as a way to turn children's own experiences into oral stories. Recordings of stories can be used as starting points for children's story-making. Although consideration has to be given to noise levels when recording, tape recording can act as a control when space is limited and it is difficult to act out a scene or short play.

Speaking and listening at Key Stage 2

At Key Stage 2, oral work can be extended to involve more complex uses of language in discussion and drama, developing children's skills in reasoning, persuading, constructing an argument or viewpoint, problem-solving and evaluating, as well as imaginative responses. Links with reading and writing can be made more extensively and at a higher level, as well as cross-curricular links. Direct work on language, standard English, accent and dialect, can also be carried out (NC English 1999, KS2 Speaking and Listening).

Responding to stories, poems and non-fiction texts will form a large part of oral work at Key Stage 2. Many of the ideas and techniques discussed at Key Stage 1 can be extended with appropriate texts; for example, the 'tell me' approach can be used with a range of relevant authors, such as Ann Fine, Dick King-Smith, William Mayne and Philippa Pearce. Rather than making this a separate section here, links to texts (both fiction and non-fiction) will be included as part of other oral work. Cross-curricular links and interactive strategies, including drama and other performing arts, are all stressed in the new Professional Standards for QTS.

Reading, writing and drama

As at Key Stage 1, starting points for imaginative and dramatic writing at Key Stage 2 can be a discussion of stories, poems, objects or photographs (see examples in Key Stage 1 section). Cross-curricular links can also be made, as illustrated in the next example, which uses story, role-play and drama as ways into the development of empathy in a history topic.

Classroom story

A Year 3 class was working on the Victorians, and their teacher read parts of Dorothy Edwards's A Strong and Willing Girl, in which a parlourmaid tells stories about her life in service. In preparation for a visit to a local Victorian manor house which included an 'upstairs-downstairs' role-play, a visiting drama teacher took on the role of Lizzy the servant girl, and enacted a short scene about her work. The children were asked to think about who the character was, what she was doing, and what she was feeling (the scene had shown Lizzy upset and angry about an event in the house), and then to brainstorm questions which they could ask her in a 'hot seating' session. This led on to the children devising plans about what Lizzy should do next to solve her problem, and improvising short scenes around their ideas. They then wrote imaginary letters home to Lizzy's Mum (as if Lizzy could write), describing events and feelings. After the outing to the manor house, the drama teacher returned to lead a whole-class simulation exercise in the hall in which the children set up a Victorian household. Role cards and instruction sheets were written by the children to denote the different roles and jobs they had seen and tried out on their visit, and the drama teacher took on the role of housekeeper, using a bell as a control device to call the household together for important meetings (NC English, KS2 S and L 4 and 11; NLS Y3, Term 3, text level 5 and 12).

Much useful and enjoyable oral work at Key Stage 2 can be undertaken about the process of drafting and redrafting children's writing (NC English, KS2 Writing). For factual writing, everyday instructional texts such as recipes and timetables (NLS Y3, Term 2, text level 12–17), or persuasive texts such as advertisements and letters to the press (NLS Y4, Term 3, text level 16–25) can form the stimulus for group discussion and writing. Once a first draft of the writing is produced, children can work with response partners in order to identify features for improvement.

For example, the children in a Year 4 class worked in pairs, using a work card to help. The children took it in turns to read their work aloud while their partner listened carefully. They were asked to consider and discuss the following kinds of questions about the writing:

- **Do you think the writing is interesting/enjoyable?**
- **Is there anything missing in the piece?**
- **Can you suggest any helpful words or expressions?**
- **Can you suggest a more suitable beginning or ending to the piece?**
- **Do you think it is too long or too short?**
- **Can anything be missed out?**
- **Has the writer written what he/she was asked to do?**

These questions can be altered according to the particular focus and purpose of the writing; for example, work on characters and story structure can emphasise questions about characterisation and the stages of the story (NLS Y4, Term 1, text level 1–3, 9–12). The activity encourages pupils to listen and express their views clearly, to work co-operatively and independently, and to develop their ideas about writing and responding to writing (NC English, KS2 S and L, 2b, d and e).

Response partners are a good way into more formal presentations to a large group, which can seem daunting without prior experience in a more protected setting. Once the children are used to trying out pair work, they can move on to more complex oral activities such as 'jigsaws'. In this, the children are divided into 'home' groups in which each pupil is allocated a specific task (e.g. finding out about different aspects of life in Roman Britain). The children with the same tasks from each home group come together into 'expert' groups in which they pool information about their topic, either independently or guided by the teacher. Once they have completed their tasks, the children return to their home groups to report back their findings. The idea of the child as expert is related to Dorothy Heathcote's dramatic device 'the mantle of the expert' (Heathcote and Bolton 1995), in which the roles are reversed in a drama and the children are more knowledgeable than the teacher; for example, the teacher is a town planner who wants to develop a site, and the children are archaeologists who know that a Roman villa is buried beneath it (Heathcote and Bolton, 1995). An example is given in the next section.

Discussion groups can also be the basis of oral work that comes together in a class presentation. This could be through the scripting and performing of a short dialogue or play (NLS Y4, Term 1, text level 5, 6, and 13; Y5, Term 1, text level 5, 18–20). It could also be in the preparation, writing and presenting of a radio or television documentary.

Classroom story

Making a documentary
A small rural primary school was celebrating its centenary and used the opportunity to carry out a number of activities related to the school and its history. The Year 5/6 class did some research about this by reading the school log book and interviewing parents, grandparents and other old people in the village who were former pupils of the school. Out of this came the start of a television documentary. The teacher divided the class into groups and each group worked on one item for the programme. There were two overall presenters who acted as continuity for the items, as well as presenters, interviewers or performers within each item. One group video-recorded interviews with former pupils and with people who worked in the school (e.g. headteacher, caretaker, secretary, dinner ladies). Two groups re-enacted events described in the log book or in interviews. Another group improvised a school scene from Laurie Lee's Cider With Rosie, *set in a rural school in the early 1900s. The final group acted as collators, providing presenters, a linking script and footage of the current school, and camera crew for some groups. Story boards and cue cards were made, and the final script was word-processed. The completed documentary, which took nearly half a term using some literacy hours and topic time, was presented in a special assembly to the school and an invited audience (NC English, KS2 S and L, all aspects; NLS Y5, Term 1, text level 5, 18–20; Y6, Term 1, text level 1, 2 and 9).*

Learning about language

The National Literacy Strategy has made the teaching of language, standard English and the structure of language explicit from the early teaching of phonics in Reception to higher level work on word, sentence and text structures in Years 5 and 6. Oral work at Key Stage 2 can address language and how it works directly through a range of activities (NC English, KS2 S and L 5 and 6). For example, in Years 4 and 5, simple pair exercises can be set up to explore accent, dialect and *register*, through comparing role-plays of informal telephone conversations with a friend to more formal communications with doctors, banks and businesses. In Year 6, detailed language investigations can be carried out through constructing language autobiographies, in which pupils talk to a partner about their own language background or analyse the language, accents and dialects used in a variety of television soap operas, for example *East Enders* (Cockney), *Brookside* (Liverpool), *Coronation Street* (Manchester), *Byker Grove* (Geordie), *Neighbours* (Australian) (NLS Y6, Terms 1 and 2, sentence level 2).

Differences in language and register can also be approached through drama (Clipson-Boyles 1998). By taking on roles, children draw on their often unconscious knowledge about language to use different ways of speaking. The teacher can be helpful in modelling this through teacher-in-role. It is important to stress that neither the teacher nor pupils need to be good actors. In Dorothy Heathcote's words, it is more a question of 'donning an attitude' (Heathcote and Bolton 1995), which teachers do all the time in the classroom! An example is shown below which also brings in problem-solving and listening to viewpoints.

Classroom story

Problem-solving drama

A Year 4 class was studying volcanoes as part of a Geography topic, and building on work done on map-making. They had read parts of William Mayne's Low Tide, *in which the effects of a tidal wave on a community are vividly portrayed. The teacher set up a whole-class improvisation in which he took on the role of village elder (rather than leader) within a community that lived near a volcano. The crops were failing and there were warning signs that the volcano might erupt soon. The elder brought some evidence (e.g. pieces of rock, earth samples, plants) to a village meeting. Addressing the villagers in a formal way ('My friends, I have called this meeting to discuss an important matter'), he asked the children in role as village experts (farmers, geologists, plant specialists) to express their views as to whether they should stay and risk the volcano destroying them, or leave and find a safer place to rebuild their community. The children took it in turns to speak and express their point of view, echoing the formal register used by the elder (e.g. 'I have lived in this village all my life and I know from the stories of my father and mother that these signs mean danger'). A lively discussion followed about the meaning of the signs and what this meant for the future of the community. The elder summed up the mood of the meeting and the views expressed. The villagers had decided to leave, and the drama ended with the villagers returning to family groups to make plans for their departure and decide what they should take with them. Out of the drama, the children were asked to reflect on their drama experience, and to write a diary entry to record their feelings about leaving the village (NC English KS2, S and L, all aspects; NLS Y4, Term 1, text level 6; Term 2, text level 4 and 13; Term 3, text level 1 and 11).*

Using language to formulate an argument and express different viewpoints can also be done through the more traditional channel of debates. These provide clear structures for teachers and pupils alike, and enable views to be prepared and scripted in advance. Pupils can practise the techniques of persuasion with pair work (e.g. marketing phone calls) as well as letter writing (NLS Y5, Term 3, text level 12 and 17). There are many variations on this theme, using a dramatic slant. For example, trial scenes also provide a framework within which different viewpoints and arguments can be put forward forcefully and persuasively. With a bit of imagination, trials can be set up to fit many topics (e.g. a Roman trial, a medieval trial, a Victorian trial...), but obviously these all need researching in advance so that the structure and roles are appropriate to the period and setting. The structure of a formal meeting is also a good one to use in a variety of contexts, such as the volcano-threatened village discussed above, and enables the teacher to establish clear frameworks for behaviour. Another example based on real-life events is as follows.

Classroom story

Community meeting

The teacher of a Year 6 class used the example of a nearby site due for demolition to combine work on persuasive argument with consideration of differing needs in the local community. The class visited the site, which consisted of some derelict land and a bingo hall that was up for sale. In groups, the pupils discussed and prepared questions arising from the visit, and then interviewed local shopkeepers and residents in order to obtain their views on the future of the site. Using the notes and recordings they had made, the pupils decided on roles which represented the different interest groups involved (e.g. developers, residents, shopkeepers, media, the council) and prepared arguments which those people could put forward at a community meeting. They also consulted local papers to see what kinds of articles or letters were written about local issues. After much preparation through discussion and writing, the class set up the meeting, which the teacher chaired in the role of a local councillor. The developers were asked to make a presentation about their proposals (to turn the site into a leisure centre) and then each person put forward their view. The discussion opened out into a heated debate about the issues, at the end of which a vote was taken, and the developers were asked to modify their plans in accord with the community's wishes (NC English, KS2 S and L, all aspects; NLS Y6, Term 2, text level 15-20).

Developing talk – points to remember

The oral activities outlined during the chapter need to be planned carefully, and chosen to match the age, abilities and experience of the children. Some activities will need to be developed slowly after simpler preparatory exercises. For example, it is hard to expect a class or a teacher to embark on a full-scale drama simulation without building up slowly with prior pair or group role-plays. Choose approaches and styles which suit you and the children, and also fit in with other literacy work being planned that term.

Some of the work described above needs careful handling and a sensitive approach on the part of the teacher. Again, prior work on developing pupils' listening skills and respect for others' viewpoints can help when dealing with emotive issues. Be encouraging to pupils who are just beginning to have the confidence to talk in the classroom. There is nothing worse than saying that a child's tentatively spoken words are wrong, but they may need help to improve the way they express themselves. There is also nothing more rewarding than seeing a child who has previously been withdrawn begin to express him or herself with confidence. Through oral work and drama, many children who in other contexts lack the ability to express themselves (e.g. in written work) find a voice and an ability to work in an imaginative and often powerful way.

As teachers, have the confidence to try out some of the drama ideas described. Many teachers are scared at the mention of drama, and yet they may tell and read stories with expression and meaning. It is only a small step further to take on a role within a drama situation or set up a group improvisation.

Speaking and listening :

a summary of key points

▬ *Talk is central to learning and can be developed from the earliest stages.*

▬ *Useful approaches involve rhymes, imaginative play, traditional stories and responding to texts.*

▬ *Drama is a key context through which speaking and listening can be developed.*

Further reading

Chambers, A. (1993) *Tell Me: Children, Reading and Talk*. Glos.: Thimble Press.

Clipson-Boyles, S. (1998) *Drama in Primary English*. London: David Fulton.

Grainger, T. (1997) *Traditional Storytelling in the Primary Classroom*. Leamington Spa: Scholastic.

Professional Standards for QTS

→ **3.1.3, 3.3.8**

Section 3 of the Professional Standards for Qualified Teacher Status requires that you can choose, prepare and manage the use of a range of resources for teaching English. This involves your being able to use effectively the physical learning space, prepare and manage any tools or materials which are appropriate to your teaching objectives, and use ICT effectively.

The Handbook accompanying the Standards clarifies these requirements and you will find it helpful to read through the appropriate section of this Handbook for further support.

Curriculum Guidance for the Foundation Stage/National Curriculum programmes of study

The Curriculum Guidance for the Foundation Stage suggests that effective language learning involves children:

- having opportunities to speak and listen and represent ideas in their activities;
- being immersed in an environment rich in print and possibilities for communication;
- using communication, language and literacy in every part of the curriculum.

The requirements of the National Curriculum are as follows:

In speaking and listening pupils should be given opportunities to:

- talk for a range of purposes;
- consider how talk is influenced by the purpose and by the intended audience;
- listen carefully and show their understanding of what they see and hear by making relevant comments;
- participate in drama activities, improvisation and performances of varying kinds;
- communicate to different audiences and reflect on how speakers adapt their vocabulary, tone, pace and style.

In reading pupils should be:

- given extensive experience of children's literature;
- encouraged to develop as enthusiastic, independent and reflective readers;
- be introduced to and read a wide range of sources of information.

The material read should cover a wide range of categories.

In writing pupils should be:

- **helped to understand the value of writing as a means of remembering, communicating, organising and developing ideas and information, and as a source of enjoyment;**
- **given opportunities to write in response to a variety of stimuli and for varied purposes;**
- **taught to organise and present their writing in different ways;**
- **given opportunities to write for an extended range of readers.**

The National Literacy Strategy

The National Literacy Strategy is a text-centred programme with focused objectives at text, sentence and word level which develop language use, language study and learning through language. It makes a number of organisational and resource demands on teachers.

Introduction

Organisation for the English curriculum is about making sure that pupils have the most effective environment for their language and literacy learning, both inside and outside the literacy hour and in the wider context of the teaching of English. This means making key decisions about the way you organise your classroom, and being creative and flexible in your planning, so that you can set up the best possible arrangements for learning. Successful organisation is, however, about more than planning appropriate lessons. It is about sharing your enthusiasm for English by creating a classroom which offers pupils opportunities to make speaking, listening, reading and writing an enriching part of their everyday school life.

This chapter aims to help you to make decisions about the use of space, time and resources, and offers you ways of thinking about how you can organise groups of pupils for different aspects of English teaching at Key Stages 1 and 2. You can implement ideas imaginatively in *any* classroom, whether you teach in an old Victorian building or a modern open-plan unit. The ideas are also applicable to classrooms for all ages of primary children. You can decide how to vary the content of activities so that they are appropriate for your particular class.

The chapter begins by discussing the general organisation of the classroom to support literacy learning, taking account of the available space, the organisation of time, and the use of other adults in the classroom. It then focuses specifically on the organisation and resourcing of the classroom for the teaching and learning of speaking and listening, reading and writing.

Organising the classroom space

Planning an exciting and stimulating school and classroom environment that supports and extends opportunities for English is a challenge. Many of us have seen large unpromising Victorian school buildings, whose walls and classrooms were never designed with displays or group work in mind. With some imagination, these can be transformed into language-rich, colourful and animated environments by teachers and pupils with energy and vision.

Each school year teachers have the luxury of 'starting afresh', transforming their empty classroom into an environment that promotes learning and reflects the curriculum back to the pupils. It is often helpful to create an outline of what you want. Bear in mind that the environment is for pupils to use and to learn in. They should feel at ease when they are reading, writing, discussing, exploring, touching, listening, asking questions, solving problems and making decisions. Getting pupils interested in their environment also means helping them to take responsibility for feeding pets, watering plants and tidying displays, so that they develop a pride and sense of ownership over their classroom. Pupils can devise a simple rota system showing the monitors for the week and listing the duties involved. Groups of pupils can work together drawing up instruction sheets that show how often plants should be watered and how much light they need. Displays may need information sheets and labels that could be researched and written by pupils during the literacy hour group activities.

When you take up your first post you may find it useful to make a plan of your room, initially by marking in those fixtures that are permanent. Using this bare outline you can experiment, deciding where you want particular areas that are concerned with language and literacy learning. These include an area for shared activities in the literacy hour, a library or book corner, a listening area, a writing area and a role-play drama or dressing-up area. Some of these areas may already be designated in your room; you will not be able to move carpets, shelving and pinboards, but there are nevertheless things you can do to organise sensibly. For example:

- **put noisy activities away from the library and listening areas;**
- **cordon off quiet areas with dividers made from moveable bookshelves or trolleys;**
- **check that the listening area is close to plug sockets and has space for a table and chairs;**
- **check that your computer area is close to plug sockets and away from messy activities such as sand and water play and art work;**
- **make sure that all areas can be used as active working spaces as well as for displays by providing appropriate furniture.**

Remember that you can change environments that you have developed at the start of the year in response to the needs of the pupils and their curriculum. You can also exchange resources with other teachers in your age phase. Moveable furniture might at one time provide facilities for group work and at another time be used for individual, group or whole-class activities.

A community space for the pupils

Many primary classrooms have a carpeted area where pupils can sit as a group. Identify the community area in your classroom and cordon it off if possible with bookshelves and trolleys. This will mark it out it as a visibly important meeting place for the class and a focus of shared activity, including whole-class and plenary sessions in the literacy hour. Remember even in the best organised classrooms, chairs and tables have a habit of moving onto the edge of the carpeted area and the community space can get smaller and smaller – so make sure it is always there to be used.

If your room is particularly small you might not be able to designate part of the area for shared activities, and pupils might have to remain seated at their tables during whole-class shared activities during the literacy hour and at other shared times. If this is the case you will need to ensure that all pupils can see the texts you use. Enlarge them on computer, or prepare an overhead transparency. If this is not possible, write the text legibly by hand on a flipchart or whiteboard.

The role-play/playspace area

How you set this area up will depend on the age and experience of the pupils. Many Key Stage I classrooms have an area set aside for home play, with chairs, a table, cooker, washing machine, dressing-up materials and so on. Printed texts can be put in here too so that children can incorporate them into their play (e.g. magazines, telephone directories, comics, calendars, recipe books – the kinds of print pupils are likely to see around them at home, both in English and in the child's first language if this is not English. (Ask parents to bring in examples of the kinds of print their child sees and uses at home.) Pupils can use this area for writing, so make notebooks and paper available for messages and shopping lists, and provide calendars to write on and forms that can be completed.

Some of the most successful and lively role-play areas are set up by the pupils as a result of something they have become involved in – a café, a railway station, a shop, or a scene from a book the class has enjoyed specifically or has studied as a literacy hour text. Changing the setting gives opportunities for you to introduce new kinds of language and print for pupils to read and write; for example, in a railway station pupils can design and make signs, labels, tickets and timetables. The café scenario gives opportunities for reading and generating signs, menus, order forms and recipes. Businesses and supermarkets are often generous in providing schools with forms, advertisements, price lists and so on. If appropriate, you can put computers, typewriters and telephones in this area to encourage different forms of writing and talking. Sometimes the role-play theme can extend across the whole classroom so that it becomes transformed into a jungle or a medieval castle. Pupils can be instrumental in this transformation, using layout sheets to design each element and taking responsibility for its coordination.

It is less likely that such transformations will take place at Key Stage 2, but as part of the literacy hour activities you can organise older pupils to write their own play scripts or research areas of interest. These can be linked with visits to museums or heritage centres. Use drama sessions too so that pupils can act out their ideas or carry out group role-play.

Puppets

A selection of different puppets, either bought or home-made, will encourage imaginative play and creative language use based on pupils' own experiences or their own re-tellings of favourite stories. Key Stage 2 children can use puppets to act out plays you have read during the literacy hour and rehearse the scenes during independent group work. Once pupils are familiar with the format of such texts, encourage them to write their own plays during guided writing, performing them during shared reading or the plenary session of the literacy hour. You do not need elaborate puppet theatres – pupils can kneel behind a table with a curtain draped in front if they want to perform their play. Simple puppet sets can be made with stick puppets inside a cardboard box with slits up each side.

Displaying some of the puppets will tempt pupils to pick them up and use them, and in many classrooms they become a favourite extension activity. Attractive containers clearly labelled with the names of the characters or puppets stored inside, together with copies of favourite books, are also popular. Pupils do like to create their own characters as well, so provide appropriate materials to enable fresh puppets to be made. You can quickly and easily produce shadow puppets and scenery with the aid of an overhead projector.

Storysacks

These consist of large cloth bags containing a picture-story book with all kinds of support materials – soft toys for the main characters in the book, props to illustrate the theme or the scenery, an appropriate non-fiction book which relates to the story (for example, 'The Three Bears' storysack would contain an information book about bears). The sack will also contain an audio-tape of the story and a language game based on the story. Storysacks can be professionally produced or home-made.

Displays

Two-dimensional displays are often the first things that children notice in the classroom. Walls covered with bright cheerful paintings and posters or advertisements create a warm and inviting atmosphere. Many of these displays are not only a celebration of the children's achievements but also have an important function in the curriculum. Some of the ways in which displays extend English curriculum activities are as follows:

- *The investigative area.* **Many schools set aside a particular place, either in a corridor, entrance hall or classroom, for three-dimensional displays. Teachers encourage children to pick up and examine different items, such as shells, a Victorian collection (e.g. shoes, a top hat, old photos, gloves, a parasol) and things to smell (e.g. spices, a pomander or a lavender bag). Items like this can relate to a class project or to an area of interest being studied by a small group. Teachers often set such displays up themselves, but there is scope for pupils to make contributions and even to set up the display themselves. You can help children to plan the layout of such a display in guided literacy hour activities, with pupils deciding what the contents of the display might be, writing the labels and seeking further information through the Internet.**

- *Wall displays.* These can consist of posters, information sheets, pictures and photographs, all of which can form the focus for shared reading in the literacy hour. Encourage pupils to create their own posters or to produce information sheets using reference books, CD-ROMs and the Internet.
- *Teacher and pupil displays.* These might be considered the natural follow-on from the formal wall display. What started as a single poster shared by the whole class can be supplemented by writing and information cards. This activity can begin as guided or independent work in the literacy hour, and carry over to other curriculum areas through pupils' drawings, paintings, databases and charts. Activities such as these have a particular value for speaking and listening because you can encourage children to share their work with the class, and to describe and exchange experiences as part of the plenary session of the literacy hour. These displays do not always have to draw on experience from a conventional text. You could put up an art exhibition drawing upon the requirements of the National Curriculum for Art as well as English. Portraits painted by a variety of artists will provide a centre of interest for the class. Invite pupils to make their own comparisons, to write exhibition reviews and to take part in a critics' forum.
- *A class noticeboard.* Use this for up-to-date class news and reports, i.e. the dinner menu, weather forecast, class news, lost and found, for sale and wanted, job applications around the school, a list of volunteers to feed the gerbil, birthdays and so on.

Working with adults in the classroom to support literacy learning

You might be fortunate enough to have adults working alongside you in the classroom, perhaps an education assistant, a parent, a support teacher, or even a student from a local secondary school on work experience. Classroom assistants or nursery nurses are permanent members of staff and may work alongside you on a regular basis. Their role in the classroom will have to be considered as part of a whole-school plan so that they are used effectively and given opportunities for their own professional development. Other adults, such as parent-helpers or secondary school students, will not be part of the regular school staff, even though they might be familiar with school routine. You will have to consider their experience and needs when you decide how they can support pupils' learning. *You may be required to show this organisation in your lesson notes.* Some areas where adult helpers can support pupils' literacy learning are:

- sitting with children in the reading area and talking with them about the books they choose to read at school or at home;
- keeping records of books borrowed from the school library for children to read at home;
- helping an independent or guided group during the literacy hour;
- telling or reading a story to a small group of children;
- listening to a child reading individually;
- making audio-recordings of stories for children to listen to;
- making books for children to write their own stories in;

- helping to put together home-made storysacks;
- observing a pupil for assessment purposes;
- helping pupils who are using ICT.

Organising time

Deciding how much time to allocate to an activity is never easy, even within a carefully-structured literacy hour, particularly if the class is new, or the activity is one you have not tried before. Here are some general guidelines.

- Give a group enough time to complete a task satisfactorily. Within the literacy hour this means making sure that tasks you set up are either ones that allow for fast but accurate work, or are planned as continuous activities throughout the week.
- Tell the pupils at the beginning of the activity when the session is going to end, so they can plan. Say something like: 'You've got 20 minutes to do this, then we'll look at the ideas your group has come up with. I'll tell you when you've got 5 minutes left.'
- Plan extension activities for more experienced groups of learners who are working independently. This will enable you to spend more time supporting a particular group of pupils during guided activities.
- Resist putting pressure on pupils who work slowly. Some need more time than others to think and discuss ideas. It is equally important to remember this during the plenary session of the literacy hour when you will have to be sensitive to those pupils who have had difficulty in completing a task.
- Find out what suits individual learners. Observe pupils at work and talk to them about their learning needs. Older pupils will often be able to tell you how they learn best. Finding out about learning needs means that you are able to plan appropriate group activities for your class and use your teacher-intensive time to best advantage.
- Build in time for groups to complete tasks, either during subsequent literacy hour sessions or in extended reading or writing time outside the literacy hour. Remember the importance of allowing pupils to complete pieces of work. Pupils become frustrated and demotivated if their work is unaccountably abandoned because they have run out of time to finish it.
- Plan to use yourself most effectively by deciding in advance which child or group you are going to work with, and what activity you will do with them. This is fundamental to planning for the literacy hour but is also important for other English activities.
- Plan carefully for the whole class, so that the pupils you are not working with directly can carry on with tasks that do not need so much input from you. Many pupils find it difficult to work independently, so it is important that you give clear instructions at the start and monitor the class regularly to forestall interruptions.
- Use classroom helpers to work with other pupils, ensuring that these helpers know exactly what they are expected to do and how you want them to do it.
- Help the pupils to learn to respect the time you have to work with each group.

Say something like: 'I'm going to work with the red group until quarter past eleven. Please don't interrupt me unless it's something very important.'

Practical task

Visit DVC Online (http://www.metamath.com/lsweb/fourls.htm) to find out more about the four learning styles in the DVC survey:

- *Visual/Verbal;*
- *Visual/Nonverbal;*
- *Tactile/Kinesthetic;*
- *Auditory/Verbal.*

Uses of ICT to support the teaching of literacy

Few teachers would say they have sufficient touch-sensitive keyboards, computers or CD-ROMs in their classrooms. You might find that you have to share your electronic hardware and software with other classes, even though many more schools have now got a separate computer suite. Whatever your situation, you will find you have to organise carefully to ensure that each pupil has an opportunity to use the computer for different purposes. Keep a register of computer use. Many schools now provide printers alongside the computer and children can use word processing packages to produce their own books, magazines or class news-sheets. With so many schools now connected to the Internet, pupils will be able to exchange e-mails with pupils not only in this country but also across the world.

It is not always possible to tell from the packages just what a program can do or even what age it is suitable for, so make your own records, including notes about the levels of difficulty offered and whether the program is best used by one, two or more pupils at a time. Some adventure games are specifically designed to provoke discussion and develop problem-solving skills. The IT coordinator in your school will give you more advice.

The Information and Communications Technology (ICT) curriculum covers not only computers and CD-ROMs, but also more conventional electronic systems – TV, radio, tape recorders, telephones, fax machines, language masters and cameras. You can use all these creatively to support and develop literacy. CD-ROMs are now available in most classrooms. Select those with interesting text, sound, animation, artwork, photographs or video that are motivating for pupils and that invite them to read and write for a range of purposes.

Several well-known publishers produce cassette recordings alongside popular books, read by accomplished actors, with music and other sound effects. Build up a collection of these and store them on the shelves alongside your books. They can provide a valuable independent activity for the literacy hour.

In addition to commercially produced tapes, make your own recordings of popular books. Encourage pupils to make their own recordings too using a variety of sound effects, and include these in your classroom library of tapes. Your class might also like to make tapes for younger pupils in the school and this gives them an opportunity to read aloud expressively for a real purpose and audience.

Many popular stories are also produced on videotape and these can form part of a school collection, giving access to texts that are difficult to read independently. Again, having copies of these available means that pupils can enjoy them over and over again and borrow them to view at home. Information tapes are also available and provide another source of reference, particularly for older pupils who are able to use them independently.

Environments for fostering speaking and listening

A supportive environment that fosters and develops speaking and listening gives children real purposes for using talk, and allows them the opportunity to investigate, develop and present their ideas. In a supportive setting, pupils will have a chance to reflect on their own uses of talk and on their role as listeners, and to work collaboratively with other children.

Practical task

Display a classroom poster similar to the one set out below to help children to become aware of the purposes of their talk, and to reflect on their own development as speakers and listeners.

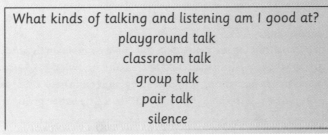

What kinds of talking and listening am I good at?
playground talk
classroom talk
group talk
pair talk
silence

Sensitive teachers do much more than 'let children talk': your role is to develop a classroom environment that encourages the growth of purposeful talk. In addition, you can support the children by being a good role model yourself. So engage the children in discussions and encourage them to listen and respond. Don't be afraid to intervene sensitively to push ideas in new directions, sometimes using new or technical vocabulary, and introducing new and complex ideas.

Be a good conversationalist and remember that children are watching and listening as you talk to their parents, to other teachers, the caretaker, the head teacher, the cleaners and to the children themselves. Don't be afraid of being hesitant and tentative yourself when you are dealing with new ideas. This will give you an opportunity to show pupils that it is perfectly acceptable to use talk to think aloud with. Part of your role is to become a good listener – so listen with care and appreciate what a child is trying to express, enlarging on their comments and feeding back ideas to them. This will show the children that you're concerned with their ideas and how they thought them through. The attention you pay to these areas will help them to take their learning seriously and give them a way of sorting out ideas when they are on their own.

Think carefully about the seating arrangements for communal whole-class sessions when you are discussing topics. Sometimes it is appropriate for you to sit on a chair with the pupils grouped around you on the carpet. At other times you might want to sit on the carpet alongside the pupils, or you might choose to sit in a circle with them. This is one of the most appropriate arrangements for whole-class discussion, because pupils can look across at each other, and at you, instead of focusing on the back of another child's head.

As well as whole-class discussions, you will want to organise children into groups for speaking and listening. Small groups that really do work together exemplify cooperation, the sharing of ideas and the justifying of opinions. In order to work like this you need to involve the group in a joint task, and suggest that they pair off into subgroups to do independent research. The discussions that take place within these small groups are beneficial because they give a greater number of pupils the opportunity to offer their opinions than whole-class sessions do. In addition, shy children often make the contributions in small groups that they are unwilling to make in front of the whole class.

Obviously the composition of these groups varies according to the needs of the task. Research has shown that groups of four generate the most talk. Some suggested groupings for specific purposes are:

- **a single-sex group to investigate a relevant issue, e.g. aspects of gender stereotyping;**
- **a group containing an 'expert' on the topic to be investigated;**
- **a group where a particular child has a good knowledge of a certain task, like word processing, editing or illustrating, and can share their expertise;**
- **a group where a shy child is given confidence by other group members.**

Some ideas for group talk are:

- *Brainstorming.* **Children in a large group, or even the whole class, contribute ideas off the top of their heads, related to a particular subject or problem. List all contributions without comment, and then ask the children to use their list to select tasks or topics for further work.**
- *Jigsawing.* **Children are organised into 'home groups' of about six to look at a topic – for example, creating a newspaper page. Each child in a home group is allocated one aspect of the newspaper page to investigate or to write, and becomes the 'expert' for that group – for example, an editor, a layout artist, an illustrator, a roving reporter, a cartoonist. The children then go into 'expert' groups from time to time, comprising all those from the home groups who have the same job description. After discussion, the 'experts' then return to their own**

home groups to discuss with the others what they have found out, and to play their part in putting together the final product before reporting back to the whole class.

- *Twos to fours.* Children work together in pairs, perhaps on a mathematical problem or a science experiment. They then join another pair to explain what they have achieved, and to compare it with the work of the other pair.
- *Rainbowing.* In this organisation, each member of the group is given a number or a colour. When the group has worked together, all children with the same number or colour form new groups to compare and discuss what they have done.
- *Envoying.* If a group needs to check something, or to obtain information, one of the group can be sent as an 'envoy' to the library or to talk to another group and will then report back. Groups can also be invited to send an envoy to another group to explain what they have done, obtain responses and suggestions, and bring them back.
- *Listening triads.* In groups of three, children take on the roles of talker, questioner or recorder. The talker explains or comments on an issue or activity. The questioner prompts and seeks clarification. The recorder makes notes, and at the end gives a report of the conversation. Next time, the roles are changed.
- *Group observers.* A group member is responsible for observing the ways in which the group works together. Using a simple guide list (which the children can devise) the observer watches and listen as the children work. The group then discusses this information, and as a result is able to review its work.

You can also use the tape recorder to support speaking and listening. Set up a tape recorder so that pupils can listen to stories and poetry they know and like. If you have a headphone set, several pupils will be able to listen at the same time – a good reason to buy several copies of the same book, so the group can all follow the text together. Make sure there is space for three or four pupils to sit comfortably and to operate the tape recorder. A listening centre can contain a selection of audio-cassette recordings of fiction, poetry, plays and non-fiction texts – some professionally pro-duced and others recorded by you, other adults or the pupils themselves. Make these recordings available for pupils to listen to alongside books during independent time in the literacy hour, and at other times too.

Using the recorder to record group discussions can provide a valuable activity for inde-pendent work in the literacy hour, because pupils can record their talk and prepare presentations. The use of the tape recorder changes the dynamics of a conversation, because pupils know that what they say will be given permanence, and can be repeated over and over again. This changes – and frequently enhances – the quality of the talk because they have to think carefully about what they are going to say and how they are going to say it. If pupils are not used to having their voices taped they need to experiment to overcome any embarrassment felt at hearing their recorded voices for the first time. Here are some more suggestions for using the tape recorder:

- tape pupils' contributions to discussion and invite them to listen afterwards to what they have said, and perhaps to transcribe part of it. Encourage them to examine their own contributions and to discuss what 'written down' talk looks like, and how it differs from formal written English;

- organise pupils to make a tape relating to the main literacy hour text. These tapes can form part of a reference collection together with books on the same theme;
- give pupils an invitation to create and record stories, their own and those already published. Remind them that when they are reading aloud they need to read expressively. Give them an opportunity to practise reading the text with sound effects to a group of pupils or to the whole class before making the final recording. Stories are often enhanced by the use of sound effects and once pupils are used to recording, they may want to include sounds on their tape. Working in pairs, encourage the pupils to scan the text they have chosen to discover where sounds would be most effective and to experiment to find the most appropriate ones;
- ask pupils to create listening games by recording sounds around the environment and asking others to guess what they are;
- organise pupils to record sound journeys inside and outside the school buildings and to present these to the class;
- organise pupils to interview people around the school, such as the caretaker or secretary, other teachers, governors, the headteacher, on particular themes;
- use one of the group's tape recordings as your main literacy hour text. Play it to the class in shared reading or writing time, and use it to generate written language;
- invite pupils to create their own radio programmes, based on what they have enjoyed listening to;
- ask pupils to devise advertisements to publicise school events using language to persuade and cajole.

Creating an environment to support writing

Try to develop an assigned space in the classroom where a group of pupils can write, either during guided or independent writing sessions or outside the literacy hour, with everything to hand. Set aside one or two tables alongside a word processor and provide different-sized paper, pencils, felt-tip pens, crayons, rulers, envelopes, and perhaps a stapler, scissors, glue and paste. Put an alphabet chart close by and a suitable dictionary and thesaurus. Provide a message board so that pupils can write letters to each other or put up news items.

Children learn about the different forms of writing by observing the kinds of writing that adults and children engage in around the school, having other people share this writing with them for different purposes, and by having opportunities to try out this writing for themselves. This means that your writing environment needs to have examples of various kinds of writing (posters, home-made books, letters, book reviews, maps, recipes, scripts, stories, poems, advertisements, and so on.) Display these at eye-level for the children to read. Displays of stimulating and exciting writing invite children to write in ways that are significant and hold meaning for them.

With the children's help, draw up lists of the various readers they can write for – you, other teachers in the school, children in their class or in other classes, the caretaker, the headteacher, their parents and relations, the cooks, penfriends, authors of books they have enjoyed, their Member of Parliament, sportsmen and women, and so on. Discussion about readership will help children to become aware of the language they should use when they are writing with a particular reader in mind.

Most pupils are used to having a choice of writing implements – pencils, biros, felt-tip pens, or crayons – but are often given only standard size paper to write on. Provide a range of paper from very small to A3, including lined paper and assorted shapes and colours. The variety may inspire the reluctant writer and capture the imagination of the creative. Young children may improve their manipulative competence by experimenting with fat and thin felt tips and chunky pencils, and different types of writing instruments offer older pupils the chance to develop their calligraphy skills. Fountain pens, bullet nosed and wedge shaped felt tips create quite different lines. Display examples of writing styles from writing patterns, from Marion Richardson and italic to illuminated manuscripts.

Organising a supportive environment for the teaching and learning of reading

The book corner

This space has two purposes: it will be both a library and a place where pupils can go when they want to browse or read; so plan for both. In a small classroom the community space often doubles as the library and this is another function that needs to be taken into consideration. Provide opportunities for pupils to visit this area outside shared activity time so that they can browse or sit and read quietly. This kind of activity helps them to develop the reading habit, and is particularly for pupils who are unable to read at home.

How you furnish this area will depend on materials and space available and on your and the pupils' ideas of design. Bookshelves are often used as partitions to define the book corner and to make it private and cosy. Test the shelves for stability – rescuing a child from underneath a bookstand knocked over by some boisterous role-play is not funny. Remember, the emphasis is on cosiness, comfort and safety.

To a large degree the type of shelving you use will probably have been decided for you but think carefully about how you use it. Plastic covered wire shelving is commonly used but there can be problems if you use it to store large soft covered books, for these tend to flop over and become permanently curved. Put hard-backed books there instead and use slanted shelves for paperbacks. There are units specifically designed for storing big books, though the inevitable size of these means that you will need to consider where they should be placed.

Many children say that their favourite place to read is in bed, because it is warm, cosy and private, so try to set up similar conditions in your book corner. A carpet or rug, scatter cushions and beanbags are ideal for children to sit on. Small settees or comfortable chairs are always popular with young readers (parents may donate chairs they no longer need). Decorate the area with plants and posters – ask your local children's bookshop for these – and display posters the pupils have made themselves to adver-tise books. You could run a special 'Book of the Month' display linked to a project or particular area of interest in the class and include a section of home-made books pub-lished in the classroom by the children themselves.

Organising and displaying books

You will want to have a varied range of reading matter, including literature of different kinds, poetry, non-fiction, and books made by the pupils themselves. Books used as lit-eracy hour texts should be on display so that children can borrow or browse through them. Some teachers exchange books with another class each term, so there is always a fresh selection for the children. In addition, you will probably be able to choose some books to keep for one year from the Schools Library Service in your area.

How you organise and display these books will depend on the space available, the pupils' reading experiences and interests, and the number and type of books you have. Some teachers ask pupils to help categorise and display the books, exploring and developing a system that suits their needs. Displaying books with their front covers visible helps to make the book corner attractive and inviting at both Key Stages. This kind of display makes it easier for inexperienced readers to choose books, because they are drawn to the title and the cover illustration. They will instantly be attracted to old favourites, and excited about picking up new and interest-ing titles. Here are some suggested ways of organising books:

- **by author's surname;**
- **by genre, e.g. humour, adventure, animal stories, poetry, folk tales, historical novels, picture-story books;**
- **by clearly recognised publisher's sets that children are familiar with, e.g. Collins Beginner Books, Ladybird retellings of fairy tales;**
- **by kinds of information, i.e. field guides, reports, auto/biographies, diaries, instructions and recipes;**
- **by homework sections that link to particular subjects or themes.**

Setting up a lending library

Many schools have a main library from where children borrow books to take home. In addition, it is sometimes helpful to set up your own class borrowing system, particu-larly if you are not able to spend time reading individually with children. A well-organised borrowing system is particularly important for younger children, because they frequently read a book in a single evening. A class library means these children can change their books every day if they wish. It also acts as an informal way of bringing parents into the classroom as they help pupils make their choice. Letting them borrow from the class library obviously means that you need a good supply of books, if it is not to be too depleted, and a system that records the borrowers. A ticket inside each book or kept in a file box and simply requiring the pupil to write his/her name is usually sufficient. When the book is returned then the pupil's name can be crossed off. The initial organisation may take some time to develop but with patience the benefits outweigh the disadvantages and parents and children can enjoy stories together. Book reviews written when children have enjoyed books at home – an ideal homework task – can be kept in the library area. You can demonstrate how to write a review in shared or guided writing time. Remind pupils that the purpose of reviews is to inform others and to help them to select books for themselves.

Reading displays

Include in your displays those books you have used as literacy hour texts as well as books that relate to a current television serial the children are viewing at home or at school. Books by a particular author who has visited the school during book week (see below) are always popular. Texts that follow a topic you are covering are worth displaying too. Invite children to display books that they have read and enjoyed at home, together with a review of the book saying why they enjoyed it.

Organising a book week

Many schools organise 'book weeks' where they invite published writers and poets to meet the children and talk to them about their writing. Although many authors may charge for their visits, others enjoy meeting their readers and may come for a nominal fee. It is worth writing to publishers saying who your children's favourite authors are and which books they particularly enjoyed. Even if they do not sponsor someone to visit your school they may send free publicity, such as badges, posters and bookmarks.

Using environmental or public print to support reading

Your reading resources should ideally include texts other than books – posters, lists and notices, the dinner menu, a weather chart, a rota for feeding the animals or watering the plants. These are all a part of class reading, so make use of them and refer to them. Sometimes you might even want to use an important notice as your literacy hour text because it contains points you want specifically to discuss.

Children are familiar with a great deal of print they see around them at home and in their community before they even come to school – food labels, TV titles, advertisements, instructions, newspapers, catalogues, calendars, magazines, comics, birthday cards, invitations, letters, bills, tickets, crosswords, coins, bank notes, car number plates and shop names. Such texts are woven into children's everyday lives and can be used successfully to support reading in the classroom. You could, for example:

- **take photos of the print that children see around them near school and put the photos into a book;**
- **discuss these with the children and write captions together in shared writing time;**
- **organise pupils to make their own alphabet books of food wrappers;**
- **collect different tickets used locally (on trains, buses, at the cinema and so on) and put these into a transparent photograph wallet so that children can read both sides of the tickets and talk about the text together.**

Resources for shared and guided reading

In addition to your chosen literacy text, you will need a selection of resources for teaching reading during the literacy hour. These will include an easel or frame of some kind to display your big book, a flip chart, a pointer, an overhead projector, sets of magnetic letters (upper and lower case), whiteboards and word or letter fans and word wheels for the pupils to use. Resources for guided or independent reading will include sufficient copies of the text you are studying (or photocopies of the appropriate page/s), pencils/highlighter pens, ICT, a tape recorder, a language master.

Choosing books

Your choice of books, both reading scheme and non-reading scheme, will depend on the National Literacy Strategy objectives you are working to, and the genres laid down in the National Curriculum for English at Key Stages 1 and 2. Read as many books as you can – this is really the only way of knowing them in detail. There are, however, several journals that review children's books, such as *Books for Keeps*, *The School Librarian* and *Signal*.

Here are some general features of different kinds of texts for your classroom. We suggest that you use the general criteria set out below together with the more detailed list for each year group, set out below.

FICTION

Choose books that use language in exciting and challenging ways, with a powerful story to tell, by authors who know how to write well for children. Look for picture books where the text and illustrations come together to make the meaning whole, such as *Rosie's Walk* by Pat Hutchins, and for wordless books where the story is carried entirely through the pictures, such as *The Snowman* by Raymond Briggs. Children love funny books, so include ones with plenty of humour. The comic strip format of books like Raymond Briggs's *Father Christmas* series appeals to the reluctant reader as well as to the enthusiast. Choose books with plenty of repetition for the younger reader, such as *Mr Gumpy's Outing* by John Burningham. Books that are serialised on television are popular, so be aware of them, both on educational TV and the main channels. Stories can be used to advantage to introduce or enrich project work. Children gain a sense of history through reading a book set in the past or one that crosses time, such as *Tom's Midnight Garden* by Phillippa Pearce, while science fiction offers a glimpse of the future.

Choose books with a variety of print styles and sizes, and look for stories that challenge stereotypes (race, gender, disability) in both text and illustration. Include books of different sizes, some small enough to hold in the hand, (such as the Beatrix Potter series) and others that are large enough to be shared by a small group of children.

POETRY

Choose anthologies and books by individual writers. Poets like Michael Rosen, Kit Wright, John Agard, Gillian Clarke, Jenny Joseph, Charles Causley, all write well for children. Include books of traditional rhymes and poetry from different cultures.

NON-FICTION

The non-fiction books in your school might be housed in a separate library area that serves the whole school. However, younger readers often find it difficult to choose non-fiction from such a huge collection. It might be possible for you to borrow texts from the main library for particular purposes, and you can extend your classroom collection by taking advantage of loans from the public library. The use of colour photography has dramatically raised the standard of environmental science books, for example, but be aware that where a particular detail is drawn to pupils' attention, a careful illustration is often more appropriate than a general photograph. Extracts from newspapers may also provide additional non-fiction material for the literacy hour and you can add these to your class collection.

Many children watch sophisticated television programmes about various subject areas – natural history is a good example – and they need books that excite them and take their knowledge forward. You might consider that it is better to buy one expensive and beautiful book on birds, written by someone who knows and cares about the subject, than to buy several smaller books which begin by telling the reader, 'This is a bird'! If you work closely with a colleague you could share the cost of this type of book and build up a collection. In line with the National Literacy Strategy's objectives for working with non-fiction texts look for books with a contents page, an index and a glossary, and a list of books that tell the reader what to read next for more information.

Instruction books (kite-making, miniature gardens, cookery, making puppets, simple science experiments, etc.) are popular and help children to read in different ways for a range of purposes. For these to be really effective children need to be able to borrow them to take home or to find the right material in the classroom to carry out the instructions properly.

PUPILS' OWN BOOKS

Have a collection of books published in the classroom and written by the pupils themselves. Produce these as professionally as you can using a word processor and encourage the pupils to develop ICT skills by publishing their own texts. They can include a blurb and a section 'About the author'. For example, one child wrote:

> My name is David Smith. I am eight years old and I have been writing stories since I was five. My favourite author is John Burningham and I try to write the kinds of stories he writes.

His blurb read as follows:

> This story is about a little boy who finds a dog on a rubbish tip and takes him home. His mum and dad tell him he can't keep it, but can he persuade them? And what will happen to the dog if he doesn't look after it?

Features of progression in reading texts

This chapter concludes with a set of detailed criteria for fiction, non-fiction, poetry and non-fiction from Reception Year through to Year 6. It covers progression in each kind of text, taking account of objectives at word, sentence and text levels, in line with the National Literacy Strategy.

RECEPTION YEAR
- Patterned texts with a flowing rhythm and repetition of particular words and/or phrases.
- Use of rhyme in poems and stories to encourage familiarity with spelling patterns and to support prediction.
- Use of regular consonant-vowel-consonant words to introduce and support understanding of sounds and blends.
- Use of rhythmic language in poems and stories to encourage momentum and increase confidence in reading.
- Use of alliteration to encourage familiarity with initial sounds.
- Stories and poems with familiar themes.
- Simple non-fiction texts to introduce young readers to information presented in different ways (e.g. recipes and instructions).
- Illustrations that help young readers to use picture cues alongside the text to establish meaning.
- Clear layout of text and illustrations which helps pupils to understanding left–right sequencing.
- Alphabet books with lower case letters to help pupils learn the sounds and names of letters and to introduce them to alphabetical order.

YEAR I
- A wider range of stories that reflect young children's experiences and introduce a world of fantasy (e.g. modern picture books, traditional tales, stories from different cultures).
- Books by authors who use interesting and challenging vocabulary and exciting and poetic language that trips off the tongue, is easily recognised and is good to say aloud.
- A widening range of simple non-fiction texts that reflect children's interests (e.g. cooking, school, the garden, people who help us, animals, dinosaurs).
- Texts with good quality illustrations that help young readers to understand the relationship between picture and text, and give them opportunities to discuss the meaning in order to support the development of contextual cues.
- Texts with speech bubbles and thought bubbles as well as conventional narrative text.
- Alphabet books with upper and lower case letters.
- Poetry and stories with patterned rhyme and rhythm.
- Collections of nonsense rhymes with humorous word play.
- Texts with patterned and predictable language to encourage the use of grammatical (syntactic) cues.
- Simple playscripts that encourage young readers to join in and read aloud together.
- Texts with repeated vocabulary to help young readers to increase their recognition of high frequency words and CVC words.
- Texts with repeated initial letters to help young readers to increase phonic awareness of initial letter sounds.

YEAR 2

- Familiar stories with predictable language to encourage the rereading of well-known and well-loved books.
- Longer stories using literary language and more complex and sophisticated plots, that allow children to enter the world of their imagination and that encourage discussion, prediction, inference and deduction.
- Stories, poems and plays with patterned and predictable language to increase confidence, fluency and independent reading.
- Stories with an increased use of dialogue to encourage awareness of punctuation and to support reading aloud expressively.
- Picture books with complex pictures for children to look at more closely, where illustrations stimulate the imagination, including good multi-cultural images.
- Stories and poems containing words with regular phonic patterns to develop knowledge of more complex vowel and consonant blends and digraphs and long vowel sounds.
- Retellings of traditional tales that encourage children to see more than one point of view and encourage them to make links between stories.
- More complex poetry using literary language to introduce pupils to the use of figurative language.
- Anthologies of poems with an emphasis on rhyme and humour.
- Books of jokes to encourage enjoyment and humour and to introduce pupils to verbal humour.
- Non-fiction texts written in a variety of styles that increase pupils' range of experience (e.g. instructions with diagrams, photographs, labels and captions) and with features and devices to help pupils learn about how non-fiction is presented (e.g. contents page, index, glossary, headings, bulleted points).
- More sophisticated alphabet books, with upper and lower case letters, possibly with a related theme throughout, to consolidate knowledge of the alphabet and alphabetical order.
- An early dictionary to help young readers learn how to find words and their definitions and to extend their written and spoken vocabulary.

YEAR 3

- Familiar stories to encourage re-reading of well-known and well-loved books.
- More sophisticated picture-story books that deal with complex ideas and use a range of literary language.
- Contemporary stories that are more subtle and complex, dealing with emotive issues in ways that young readers can handle, and with plots and characters that readers of this age can identify with. Some of these should be longer stories divided into chapters.
- Stories that use the first-person narrative.
- Traditional stories from around the world that use rich literary language and more complex sentence structures.
- Texts that support the development of more complex spelling patterns (e.g. long vowel phonemes) and provide an opportunity for young readers to develop their knowledge of grammar (e.g. identifying adjectives).
- Non-fiction texts that extend pupils' knowledge of the world by offering sophisticated uses of language and more unusual vocabulary, including

specialised terminology, and that give readers an opportunity to see how text and illustrations work together to reveal information. These texts should also give pupils the experience of using different organisational devices, including the use of different fonts.

- A variety of poetry, in anthologies and single-authored collections, offering challenging uses of figurative language, word play and verbal humour.
- Playscripts to develop pupils' ability to read aloud with expression and take turns in their reading.
- More complex alphabet books that reinforce the alphabet and alphabetical order and help young readers to extend their vocabulary and their knowledge of grammar (e.g. tenses, punctuation).
- A dictionary that is sufficiently complex to give pupils an opportunity to learn about organisation (e.g. alphabetical order to 1st, 2nd places, use of headword and guideword).

YEAR 4

- Familiar stories to encourage rereading of well-known and well-loved books.
- More sophisticated picture-story books that deal with complex ideas and use a range of literary language.
- Short novels to give young readers the experience of reading an entire book.
- Traditional stories from around the world that encourage comparisons and introduce discussion of story structure (e.g. comparison between fables and fairy tales) and that give an opportunity to discuss the use of vocabulary drawn from different languages.
- More sophisticated contemporary stories with chapters and chapter titles and features such as first-person narrative.
- Books of jokes and riddles to read and enjoy that help young readers to explore the use and meanings of figurative language in sophisticated word play.
- Anthologies and collections of single-authored poetry that offer pupils varied styles (rhyming, non-rhyming, use of figurative language, including metaphor and simile, alliteration and onomatopoeia, a variety of layouts to stress meaning in visual terms, and sophisticated uses of punctuation to enhance meaning).
- Non-fiction texts with sophisticated features (extended narrative, captions, speech bubbles, diagrams, instructions, lists, explanations) and more complex organisational structures (contents, glossary of specialised vocabulary, index, headings, subheadings, numbered instructions).
- A more complex dictionary with many entries (2000-3000 words are recommended) giving pupils an opportunity to focus on definitions, word classes and word families to support spelling.

YEAR 5

- Longer novels, including mysteries and adventures, containing challenging vocabulary and dialogue, more sophisticated plot structures and literary devices to build tension, and move the narrative forward (e.g. time shifts, parts of the story told from different viewpoints, first-person narrative and use of the omniscient author).

- Sophisticated picture-story books that reflect the complex relationship between illustration and text and enable pupils to develop their understanding of visual literacy.
- Traditional stories from a range of cultures using more complex story structure and with rich and varied vocabulary drawn from different languages with their typical structures and use of imagery.
- Poetry using a range of styles, structures and language patterns, with varied rhymes and rhythms, and uses of figurative language.
- A wide variety of non-fiction genres, including biographies, instructional texts and extended accounts that include a range of sophisticated elements (e.g. more complex reports and recounts using specialised vocabulary, text and pictures which help children to make composite meanings, diagrams, maps, charts and labels to support meaning, clearly written advice, instructions, speech bubbles, time lines and lists of primary sources used when compiling the text).
- A good dictionary (5000–6000 words) and a thesaurus.

YEAR 6

- Stories, longer novels and playscripts, based on contemporary, historical, futuristic and fantastic themes, both hardback and paperback, containing challenging vocabulary and dialogue, sophisticated and complex narrative structures and distinctive literary devices which create suspense and move the narrative forward (e.g. links between the past, present and future, careful organisation of paragraphs and lead sentences to develop characters.
- Traditional tales that extend pupils' understanding of the literary heritage of other cultures and enable them to understand links between stories.
- Poetry with a variety of forms and styles, structures and patterns of language, that explores complex ideas in a variety of rhymes and rhythms, using humour and figurative language and sophisticated word play. These styles should include haiku, limericks, couplets, triplets, quatrains, quintets, sestets, octets. Some of these poems should lend themselves to being read aloud using intonation and expression.
- A wide variety of non-fiction genres, including biographies and autobiographies, interviews, diaries, first-hand accounts, extracts from news reports, instructional texts and extended accounts. Some of these should be explanatory and discursive texts that deal with difficult and controversial issues and put forward balanced arguments (e.g. complex reports and recounts using specialised vocabulary (supported with a wide ranging glossary) to encourage pupils to identify the differences between fact and opinion. These should also reflect widespread use of diagrams, maps, photographs, charts, graphs, footnotes and labels to support meaning, and clearly written advice, instructions, speech bubbles, time-lines and a list of primary sources used when compiling the text.
- A dictionary containing at least 10,000 words with definitions, notes on word origins and pronunciation.
- An etymological dictionary to explore word origins and derivations.
- A thesaurus.

Organising and resourcing English :

a summary of key points

- *You need to think about how you organise the classroom space for English work.*
- *You need to allow space and time to mount effective displays to stimulate and develop children's learning.*
- *You also need to think about the roles of other adults in your classroom.*
- *Time and resources are other key aspects to classroom organisation.*

Further reading

Evans, J. (2000) *The Writing Classroom*. London: David Fulton.
Goodwin, P. (1999) *The Literate Classroom*. London: David Fulton.
Phinn, G. (2000) *Young Readers and their Books*. London: David Fulton.

Professional Standards for QTS

(→) 3.2.1–3.2.7

Section 3 of the Professional Standards for Qualified Teacher Status requires that you can use a range of strategies to monitor pupils' progress in English. This involves your being able to assess their levels of achievement accurately, identify and support pupils who are working above or below their expected achievement levels, and record such information in ways appropriate to the needs of colleagues and of parents.

The Handbook accompanying the Standards clarifies these requirements and you will find it helpful to read through the appropriate section of this Handbook for further support.

Curriculum Guidance for the Foundation Stage/National Curriculum programmes of study

The Curriculum Guidance for the Foundation Stage suggests that effective teaching of language requires that practitioners observe children and use the insights gained from this to plan for the contexts in which they might best develop their speaking and listening and their understanding of reading and writing.

The National Curriculum is based around a series of level descriptors, which describe the types and range of performance that children working at a particular level should be able to demonstrate within each Attainment Target. Teacher assessment of children's progress is an essential element of effective teaching in that it enables appropriate planning for the next steps in learning. There are more formal systems of assessment at the end of each Key Stage, using standard assessment tasks.

The National Literacy Strategy

The National Curriculum for English specifies the content that all maintained schools are required to teach their pupils. The NLS goes further than this and suggests termly objectives for teaching in both reading and writing (but not in speaking and listening). Clearly teachers need to be able to monitor children's achievement of these objectives and, again, teacher assessment is an essential ingredient of effective teaching.

Introduction

Planning and assessment are the key to effective English teaching. As a teacher you need to know what a child can do and knows. You can then plan for progression. However, assessment of English is complicated because it serves many purposes and takes many forms. This chapter will consider the purposes for assessing English and then look at three main areas of assessment:

- **how the teacher can assess and record English through the academic year;**
- **the statutory assessment requirements you will be involved in for children at the end of Foundation Stage, Key Stages I and 2;**
- **the reporting of assessment to teachers and parents.**

The purposes of assessment

There are several reasons why assessments are made of children's reading, writing, speaking and listening. We shall briefly describe six of these, as follows:

1. to measure progress;
2. to diagnose difficulties;
3. to help match tasks, materials and methods to particular needs;
4. to evaluate teaching approaches;
5. to compare pupils;
6. to maintain and improve standards.

Measuring progress

Assessment measures progress. This is important to individual children and their parents, to their teachers and to the school as a whole. The main focus of *formative* teacher assessment is to measure and monitor progress against the learning objectives for English. As a result of this teachers will regularly pinpoint class targets and individual targets for children. Schools administer a *summative*, or 'snapshot', assessment to their children at the end of each year using teacher assessment, statutory tests and tasks. They then report these assessment results to parents and record the results in such a way that indicates whether children have made progress over a longer period.

Diagnosing difficulties

A further use of assessment is to identify particular difficulties in English which individual children may have. This can be done at several levels and there is a statutory procedure for diagnosing the difficulties faced by children with special educational needs. Some children who have English as an Additional Language (EAL) may simply need focused support to learn more English. As a teacher you will need to be able to mark diagnostically and use processes such as miscue analysis.

Matching tasks and materials to children

As a result of recognising children's progress or diagnosing children's problems, judgements may also be made of the kinds of differentiation, materials and teaching methods that would best fit individual children's needs. Teaching can therefore be tailored to these needs. In this way assessment feeds into planning.

Evaluating teaching approaches

One of the products of assessments of progress might be an evaluation of the teaching methods and materials experienced by the children. Assessments of children's progress are not the only source of this evaluation. Teachers will also evaluate materials and approaches on the grounds of their complexity, ease of operation and intelligibility. The extent of children's learning is, however, an important and necessary criterion for judging the success of teaching approaches. Evaluation of methods and materials will also take place on a local and national level. For instance, a Local Education Authority (LEA) might look at the statutory assessment results of its schools to evaluate the impact of electronic whiteboards in school. Nationally, the statutory assessment results are one of the factors against which the success of the NLS will be measured.

Making comparisons between pupils, schools and groups of pupils

Assessments are also used to compare pupils within the national sample, within LEAs or in smaller groups such as school or class populations. These comparisons can be made in order to reveal whether certain groups of pupils are facing problems. Recently it was noted that a national comparison of pupils in writing revealed that boys were underperforming. This has led to a national effort to improve boys' writing. Comparisons can also be made within schools and classes, to reveal whether national issues apply in a particular class or school. Such comparisons may be used as a means of allocating resources to particular groups. A school or a local authority may, for example, decide to provide extra teaching equipment or teaching help to a group of children who have been identified as having special needs.

Comparisons between schools on the basis of Statutory Assessment results are not simple, as school intakes and circumstances differ enormously. School performances are compared with 'benchmarks' of groups of schools judged to be generally similar in circumstances.

Maintaining and improving standards

Rigorous, comparable assessments allow us to know whether English standards have been maintained and improved. This information is important at a national, local education authority and whole-school level. The assessments used for this sort of measurement are the results of statutory assessment in English at Key Stages I and 2. When compared with data from baseline assessments, a measure of 'value added' – the amount of performance increase between assessments – can be made. In response to this information the government (or LEA or school) sets targets for aspects of teaching it wishes to improve. At the moment the national target for literacy is that 80% of all children should achieve level 4 in reading and writing (by 2002). The aim of this is to maintain and improve national standards.

It is apparent from the above description of the purposes of assessment that a range of interested parties have a concern with the English assessments made of children. The five main interested parties are:

- national bodies, such as QCA, representing government;
- local education authorities, who monitor and support the schools in their area;
- the individual school and its staff;
- individual teachers planning their teaching;
- the children and their parents who are actually making progress in English.

Assessment serves rather different purposes for each of these groups and a range of forms of assessment are necessary to satisfy all purposes.

Teacher assessment of literacy and oracy

There are three basic sources of data for assessing oracy and literacy:

- what children actually produce – this involves looking at writing, analysing reading aloud behaviour in one-to-one, group or shared reading, analysing what children say;
- what children actually do – observing writing processes, reading processes and speaking and listening processes;
- what children know – asking children what they know, their opinions and attitudes.

Analysing products

A great deal can be gleaned from analyses of children's language and literacy products. We shall look closely at two aspects of this: firstly at a technique for analysing the product of a child's oral reading, and secondly at the assessment of written products.

RESEARCH SUMMARY

American researchers Ken and Yetta Goodman are the theorists responsible for much of the important work related to error analysis (see Goodman, Watson and Burke, 1987 for a full account of miscue analysis). Marie Clay (1979) has looked at the reading of younger children and developed a procedure called running record, which is part of the reading recovery programme of early intervention.

According to the theory, reading errors are never simply random. Each error is caused by the interactions between a set of circumstances that include the syntactic, semantic and graphophonic cues used for reading. If a child makes errors, an observer can analyse these errors to see what cues are being used successfully and what cues need more attention. This approach to reading (and spelling) has been very useful and a running record is now part of the statutory assessment at Key Stage I.

ANALYSIS OF READING ERRORS (MISCUE ANALYSIS OR RUNNING RECORD)
Error analysis is based on the theory that the mistakes a child makes when reading aloud from a text betray a great deal about how that child is tackling the reading task. As an example, the following sentence in a reading book, 'The man got on his horse' was read by a child as, 'The man got on his house'. Because the word 'house' does not make sense in this context, it is fairly safe to assume that making sense was not the chief preoccupation of this child, who seems rather to be attending to the initial letters of the word. Another child read the sentence as, 'The man got on his pony'. This child seems to have been attending more to the meaning, even to the extent of

ignoring what the word looked like. These two children seem to have different approaches to the task of reading, which lead them to 'miscue' in different ways.

The misreading of one word is not sufficient evidence upon which to base a complete assessment. The technique of miscue analysis, therefore, uses a child's oral reading of much longer texts and tries to point out patterns in the kinds of misreadings that the child produces. It is usually carried out with the child reading from his/her normal book, and the teacher recording exactly what the child reads onto a copy of the text that she has in front of her. There are several suggested coding systems for this recording, although the exigencies of time usually mean that the simplest possible system is most effective (it is also possible to tape-record the child's reading for later, more detailed, analysis if this is required). The child may then be asked to retell the story just read, so as to provide an indication of comprehension. The miscues the child has made are then analysed by the teacher for patterns, which may indicate particular features of the child's approach to reading. To show how this technique operates we shall go through an example in more detail.

Two eight-year-old children, Gary and Robert, were asked to read aloud from a text. Their reading errors were recorded using the following system:

//	=	pausing
<u>behind</u>	=	sounding out phonically
~~the~~	=	omission
on /	=	addition
make ~~milk~~	=	substitution
C	=	self-correction

Figure 12.1 shows the record of Gary's reading and Figure 12.2 that of Robert.

Figure 12.1 A record of Gary's reading

In a hole in the // ground there lived

a // ~~hobbit~~. Not a // nasty, dirty wet
(happy C above hobbit)

// ~~hole, filled with~~ the ends of worms
(horrible C, Full, of above hole filled with)

and an // ~~oozy~~ smell, nor yet a dry,
(awful above oozy)

~~bare,~~ // ~~sandy~~ hole with nothing in it
(clean, sand above bare sandy)

to sit ~~down~~ on or ~~to~~ eat: it was a

// hobbit- ~~hole~~ and that means // ~~comfort.~~
(house above hobbit-hole, comfortable above comfort)

Figure 12.2 A record of Robert's reading

For each child the teacher completed an analysis form and these are given below.

Gary		
Original word	**What the child read**	**Likely cause of miscue**
hole	*house*	*Guessing from initial sound?* *Possibly looking forward to 'lived'.*
hobbit	*hop*	*Guessing from initial sound.*
nasty	*naughty*	*Initial sounds.*
ends	*end*	*Only read beginning of word.*
worms	*warm*	*Initial sound.*
oozy	*old*	*Initial sound.*
bare	*bar*	*Initial sounds only.*
sandy	*sand*	*Only read beginning of word.*
hobbit	*hoppy*	*Initial sounds only.*
comfort	*cold*	*Initial sounds only.*

Robert		
Original word	**What the child read**	**Likely cause of miscue**
hobbit	*happy*	*Expecting a further noun.* *Self-corrected when error realised.*
hole	*horrible*	*Initial sound? Fits tone of sentence.* *Corrected.*
filled	*full*	*Meaningful response.*
with	*of*	*Responds to meaning of previous miscue.*
oozy	*awful*	*Near synonym.*
bare	*clean*	*Follows on from dry. Possibly opposite of* *'dirty wet'.*
sandy	*sand*	*First part of word only. Meaning preserved.*
down	*–*	*Preserves meaning.*
to	*–*	*Preserves meaning.*
hole	*house*	*Initial sound? Preserves meaning.*
comfort	*comfortable*	*Preserves meaning.*

The teacher was now in a position to make an assessment of each child's reading and a statement about the kind of experiences they would now need. These assessments were as follows:

Gary does not appear to be reading for meaning. His miscues suggest attention to graphophonic cues only. This is confirmed by the prevalence in his reading of under-breath sounding out. He is over-using phonics and this material seems much too hard for him.

He needs to be encouraged to read much easier material and to approach it looking for meaning. Simple cloze material may get him to focus more on context cues. We might also use information books more. If he is interested in their subject he might be more inclined to approach them looking for meaning.

Robert clearly realises that reading is chiefly about meaning. His miscues largely suggest a concern for meaning-seeking. At times he is a little cavalier about the actual words on the page, preferring his guess, albeit usually a sensible one, to looking carefully at the words.

His attention to meaning must not be disturbed, but he needs to be encouraged to look more carefully at the words on the page. We could try getting him to read some poetry, especially out loud. Getting the words exactly right is more important in poems.

This example has hopefully shown some of the very rich insights into children's reading which the analysis of miscues can provide. A running record is very similar but also records words the child gets right. This makes it more suitable for the younger age range. Following the reading both running record and miscue analysis should be followed by a discussion about the text, so that the child's comprehension can be estimated and evaluated. This technique, in common with all assessment techniques, is never the sole source of information available to the teacher. Other sources, such as those described below, will be used to confirm, modify or enlarge on the insights gained from miscue analysis. The teacher will build up a battery of assessment techniques, each complementary to the other.

Practical task

Looking diagnostically at errors is a very important skill for you. By doing a miscue analysis you will change the way you listen to readers. You should do a miscue analysis or running record with four or five children. Either use the coding system above or use the code in the Statutory Reading Task for Key Stage 1 Teacher Handbook.

Select a passage or part of a book. Make sure it is a little difficult for the child. Select a child to read with you and tell them you would like them to read but that you will not help them. The child should do what he/she normally does if he/she gets to a difficult bit.

- *Read the text up to the passage you have selected.*
- *Ask the child to read your selected passage and mark errors in the code above.*
- *Read the rest of the story to the child.*
- *Ask the child to retell the passage and discuss it.*
- *Analyse the miscues and comprehension as shown in the discussion.*

Analysis of written products

Teachers mark and assess a great deal of writing and it cannot all be marked at the same level. When marking any work, the teacher refers to the objectives for that work. If the piece is writing of a particular text type, assessment of writing must begin with a consideration of the aims originally formulated for this piece of work. The product cannot be judged unless these are taken into account. The assessment must also take into consideration the capabilities of the children producing the work. A piece of writing may be good for one child, but well below another's capacity. The assessment should also focus on the intended audience for the writing, and whether it is appropriate for this audience.

The NLS offers teachers guidance for marking and a prompt sheet for use when thoroughly marking a piece of children's writing. This sort of piece might then to be put in a portfolio of the child's work to be used for later review of progress or reporting teacher assessment at the end of year. At times you will want to set particular writing assessment tasks and analyse the results carefully.

NLS Guidance for marking a single piece of writing

1. **Quickly read the writing for a sense of what it is about and an overall impression of how well it responds to the task set.**
2. **Decide which aspects of the analysis are most relevant/useful to you.**
   This varies depending on the age of the child (e.g. you may not expect Year 2 children to be writing very complex sentences, but you may be interested in their use of adjectives) and the nature of the task (e.g. some descriptions may contain little variation in verbs, but noun groups may be more significant).
3. **Starting with the aspects identified in point 2, read through the writing again. Notice the frequency, variety and appropriateness of the use of the selected aspect.**
   For example, are there many adjectives? Do they vary in terms of specificity/generality, common/uncommon? Do they fit in terms of formality/informality, technical/untechnical?
4. **Make a judgement about the effectiveness of the use of this aspect and tick one of the Yes/No/Partial columns.**
   For example, in an explanation, attempts to join ideas using 'when' or 'after' rather than using 'because' or 'as a result', suggests that the writer has some idea of subordination, but is not confident in using a range of subordinators. This would result in a tick in the 'Partial' column.
5. **Where the analysis has included most aspects on the sheet, look at the patterns of use emerging from columns.**
   For example, in a piece of writing there may be evidence of complex sentence construction but only partial grasp of punctuation to mark clauses. There may also be effective appeal to the reader, but little development of content and only partial use of paragraphing.
6. **Look for connections between the different aspects** (in the last example, long rambling sentences and unclear paragraph divisions may work together), **before deciding what to tackle first.**

7. **Identify an opportunity in teaching to:**
   - **revisit and extend understanding and use of those aspects in the 'Partial' column**
   - **focus clearly on any aspects in the 'No' column**

If using the sheet for analysing several pieces of writing, look for patterns across the writing as well as within one piece. You can use one sheet to record judgements on several pieces of writing.

Writing analysis sheet

Grammar *Significant features at word and sentence level*	Judgement of effective use		
	Yes	**No**	**Partial**
Sentence structure			
• simple sentences			
• complex sentences			
• variation within sentences			
• coordination			
• subordination			
Word choice			
• noun groups			
• verb choice			
• tense			
• adjectives			
• adverbs			
• pronouns			
Punctuation used to demarcate			
• sentences			
• clauses			
• phrases			
• words in lists			
• direct speech			
Organisation and effect *Significant whole text features*			
• appeal to reader			
• development of topic, content, theme			
• openings and closings			
• organisation and length of paragraphs			
• presentation and layout			

Observation

Teachers observe children working all the time. As a result of this observation they make assessments of children's abilities and attitudes, and plan future work. Yet, when asked about their methods of assessment, they will hardly ever count observation among them. Perhaps because observation is so common an activity and seems so subjective, it is very underrated in terms of the assessment information it can provide. Yet it has a great deal of potential. Its greatest strength lies in the fact that it enables assessments to be made while children are actually engaged in language work, and does not require them to be withdrawn from it into a special testing situation. It therefore enables direct analysis of the child's process of working, without which assessment must be incomplete.

To use observation deliberately as an assessment technique requires a systematic approach. It also requires some means of recording the information gained rather than relying on memory alone.

A systematic approach will involve first of all knowing exactly what one is going to be looking for. This might mean listing the skills it is hoped to assess, and preparing a checklist of them. An alternative approach is to list the activities the children will be doing, and leaving space for noted observations about their performance.

Observation can be guided by a list of points to look for, suggestions for which are given below. It is important to state that these points are not intended to be simply 'ticked off' as assessments are made. They ideally require a more qualitative response, which can be added to as more information is acquired, and, of course, revised as progress is made. The list of points is divided into three sections, each corresponding to an area of language and literacy (National Curriculum attainment targets). Neither list is intended to be comprehensive, and neither are the points intended to be read as a series of attainment statements (pace National Curriculum). They are intended as points to guide systematic observation.

READING
Does the child:

- **participate in shared and guided reading? How?**
- **select an appropriate book to read?**
- **judge when a book is too difficult?**
- **become absorbed in a book?**
- **respond to what is read?**
- **reread favourite books?**
- **retell stories previously read?**
- **use a variety of cues in reading words in shared, guided and individual reading?**
- **read silently?**
- **understand the way books and print work?**
- **have an appropriate language with which to talk about the way he/she reads?**

WRITING
Does the child:

- **turn to writing as an enjoyable activity?**
- **make independent attempts to write?**
- **write appropriately for different purposes and audiences?**
- **participate in revision activities in shared or guided reading?**
- **revise and redraft writing with or without the help of an adult?**
- **collaborate with other children in writing activities?**
- **make attempts to spell and punctuate correctly?**
- **have good habits of letter-formation etc.?**

TALKING AND LISTENING
Does the child:

- **participate in large and small group discussion?**
- **listen to others' points and respond to them?**
- **articulate ideas in a clear and appropriate manner?**
- **match his/her manner of talking to the needs of an audience?**

Probing and questioning

To find out what children think and know as they read and write you may want to have regular, possibly half-termly, conferences with individual children about their reading and writing. You will also ask them directly how they work out words, how they choose words and how they make language decisions in shared and guided reading and writing and in plenary sessions. Three types of probing questions are useful in this.

LOOKING-BACK QUESTIONS
These are of the type, 'Can you tell me how you did that?' They can be useful when looking at children's work alongside them. The children's answers to this question may well reveal a great deal about their perceptions of the processes of language. The following extract from a conversation between a teacher and seven-year-old Clare is an example of this approach. Clare has just written her version of the story of Red Riding Hood in which the heroine is menaced by an alien rather than a wolf.

Teacher: 'Oh, that's an interesting story, Clare! Where did you get the idea from?'

Clare: 'From my book. We don't have wolves here any more.'

T: 'Yes, that's right. Can you tell me how you started writing your story? What did you do first?'

C: 'Me and Joanne talked about it and … we just wrote it.'

T: 'Did you write it together?'

C: 'Well … at first we wrote the same thing … then Joanne wanted to change hers and I didn't. So we wrote different ones.'

T: 'Did you change your story at all? As you were writing it?'

C: 'I changed some words …. Emma told me how to spell them.'

T: 'Oh, Emma helped you too? What did she do?'

C: 'She read the story after I finished it. She told me my spellings.'

T: 'Yes … Now, did you plan to do anything with your story when you finished it? … Who did you want to read it?'

C: 'Put it on the wall?'

As a result of this conversation the teacher was able to make several observations about this child's approach to and expertise in language processes. Clare had clearly been able to extract information from a book and use it in another context: a fairly advanced skill for a seven-year-old. She had been able to participate in discussion both in planning her writing and in editing it. She was prepared to work on her writing collaboratively although this did not survive the disagreement with her partner. Her approach to the writing process showed some evidence of planning although this was not extensive. She was unclear about the destination and audience for her writing and saw revision purely in terms of editing spellings.

All these evaluations would require further investigation, but it is clear from this brief extract what a wealth of information the teacher was able to glean simply by asking questions that caused Clare to reflect on what she had done.

LOOKING-FORWARD QUESTIONS

An alternative kind of question can be of the type, 'Can you tell me how you will do that?' They ask children to think about their actions before they do them. It is, of course, possible that because this question makes them think through in advance what they will do, their performance is different from what it would have been without the question. The question may therefore have a teaching role, as well as being a way of seeing whether they know what to do.

Questions such as the following are of this type:

- **'When you go to the library to look for that book, can you tell me what you will do?'**
- **'Now, you are going to write your report on sports day for the school newspaper. How will you start?'**
- **'This group are going to discuss your puppet play. How are you going to make sure everyone gets a fair chance to say what they think?'**

As a result of questions like these the teacher is able both to make an initial assessment of children's approaches to the process and to prompt them in a way that may develop their thinking.

THINKING-OUT-LOUD QUESTIONS

These are of the type, 'What are you thinking as you are doing that?' They can help make children's thinking about certain tasks explicit and alert the teacher to faulty approaches. They may include questions such as:

- **'As you make notes from that book, can you tell me why you are choosing those things?'**
- **'How did you know that word said "unusual"?'**

- 'How can you work out what might come next?'
- 'Now, is your discussion going well? Have you found any problems?'

It is quite likely that, in general, teachers ask too few questions like this. In addition to providing useful information about the way children are thinking, they can have the important effect of heightening children's awareness of the way they are using language. Developing this *metalinguistic awareness* is an important task for the teacher of language and literacy.

Assessing talk

It is important to monitor and assess children's speaking and listening skills, both formatively and summatively. Approaches might include self-evaluations by children of their own talking, using similar types of question to those detailed above. Children's talking can be tape recorded for analysis by the teacher: alternatively, the teacher can take notes during discussion sessions which can be used to inform later assessments, using criteria appropriate to the purpose and focus of the activity. For summative assessment purposes, the National Curriculum level descriptions for speaking and listening can be applied.

Drama in itself can be used as an assessment tool because it often represents the presentation and review of oral (and written) work covered over a period of time. Improvised drama can also be used for assessment purposes, especially if the teacher is observing; when the teacher is in role, brief notes made immediately after the session can be used in conjunction with self-evaluations by the children.

With all assessment activities, it is important that they are integrated as far as possible with other aspects of the work, related to planning, and made transparent to the children themselves so that they are aware of what criteria are being used to assess their speaking and listening. Feeding back assessment findings is also important, so that children can make further progress.

Statutory assessment

Statutory assessment takes place at a number of points in children's development as language users. This chapter describes the requirements of baseline assessment, and at the end of Key Stages I and 2. You should look at the official materials and teacher handbooks for these assessments carefully.

Baseline assessment

In September 1998 all maintained primary schools had to adopt a scheme of baseline assessment from the list of accredited baseline assessment schemes and to inform the LEA of their chosen schemes. All children aged 4 or 5 admitted to a primary school are assessed within seven weeks of starting school, whether they enter a reception class or year I. Only children attending a designated nursery class or unit not part of the main school are excluded from assessment. These children will be assessed when they start school formally.

The assessments include a wide range of observations about children's oracy and literacy abilities and do not ask teachers to 'pass or fail' children, but rather to rate their performance on entering school.

Guidance on the statutory requirements for baseline assessment is given in the DfEE Circular 6/98 *Baseline Assessment of Pupils Starting Primary School*.

RESEARCH SUMMARY

Marie Clay, in her research into early reading, identified a series of early reading behaviours and used them to develop the 'Concepts of Print Test', arguing that beginning readers need to demonstrate an understanding of particular reading behaviours. You might want to compare the processes she identified with the information required in baseline assessment, and consider how you might build the recording of observations such as these into an early assessment of young children's reading development. Clay's (1979) key processes were:

- *understanding how to hold a book the correct way up;*
- *recognising that the words on a page carry the central message;*
- *knowing how to find the first and last parts of the story in a book;*
- *understanding that the line of print at the top of the page is to be read first;*
- *understanding that print is read from left to right;*
- *knowing that the page number is not part of the story.*

Statutory assessment at the end of Key Stage 1 and 2

At the end of each key stage children undergo two types of statutory assessment – tasks and tests which are set nationally, and teacher assessment which is reported alongside the results of tasks and tests.

The National Curriculum English tasks and tests are summative measures of the work of the Key Stage. They assume coverage of the knowledge, skills, understanding and breadth of the programme of study for reading and writing in order to meet the standards of performance described by levels 1–3 (for Key Stage 1) and 3–5 (Key Stage 2) and as appropriate for each task or test.

Statutory assessment at the end of Key Stage 1

Teachers are required to use the Key Stage 1 tasks and tests with all children to be assessed at the end of Key Stage 1 to make separate assessments of reading, writing, spelling and mathematics. The tasks must be completed between the beginning of January and four weeks before the end of the summer term (the assessment period). The tests must be completed during May.

The Key Stage 1 tasks and tests are not strictly timed. However, guide times for the administration are given in the Teacher's Guides to the tests. Funding for supply cover to help teachers complete the tasks (particularly the time-consuming individual reading) is available from the DfEE Standards Fund.

THE READING TASK

The most time-consuming task is the individual reading task involving miscue analysis of a reading of a selected book and discussion of the text. The task assesses the child's ability to read a book aloud with accuracy and discuss his or her understanding of the text, and awards levels 1 and 2, with grades C–A at level 2. The booklists from which teachers can select the reading text for the reading task are revised annually and include high-quality publications. Details of the books are available in December when the tasks are distributed to schools. Teachers are required to use a book with which the child is not familiar. The reading task must be used with all children who are judged to be working towards or within level 1 or within level 2.

Assessment of reading at level 1 is through the reading task only, and children who have achieved level 1 in the reading task *must not* be entered for the level 2 reading comprehension test – it would be demoralising and confusing for them. Teachers must use their judgement so that children who have not yet completed the reading task but are expected to achieve level 1 are not entered for the level 2 reading comprehension test.

THE LEVEL 2 READING COMPREHENSION TEST

For those children who achieve level 2 in the reading task there is a reading comprehension test for level 2. It consists of a fully illustrated story and one or more other texts with questions for children to answer on each page of a single booklet. The test awards level 2 and provides grades C–A at this level. The level 2 test provides additional and complementary information to the reading task. The test assesses the child's ability to read independently and respond in writing to comprehension questions.

THE LEVEL 3 READING COMPREHENSION TEST

For those children who do very well in the level 2 comprehension test and reading task (scoring an A) there is an additional reading comprehension test for level 3, which is based on a story booklet and a separate information booklet, together with one question booklet for children to complete. The information text for the level 3 test is presented in a separate booklet so that children's skills in reading information text and using features such as a contents list can be assessed more realistically. The test awards level 3.

THE WRITING TASK

All children undertake a writing task, which covers levels 1 to 3 at the end of Key Stage 1. It provides grades C–A at level 2. The task assesses the child's ability to communicate meaning in writing, to use punctuation and spelling accurately and to write legibly. The guidance to teachers for the administration of the writing task is very comprehensive and includes example tasks related to books on the reading task booklist. Teachers can use one of these example tasks or they may set their own task based on another book. The book must be one from the reading task booklist or another book of similar quality, which is related to work going on in the classroom at the time of the task.

THE SPELLING TEST

Children who have achieved level 2 in writing do a spelling test for levels 1–3 with the rest of the tests in May. It will allow a separate outcome for spelling at levels 2 and 3 to be reported. Children whose teacher assessment in writing is level 2 or above, or who achieve level 2 or 3 in the writing task, must be entered for the spelling test.

Statutory assessment at the end of Key Stage 2

THE LEVELS 3-5 READING TEST

All children undertake a reading test at the end of Key Stage 2. This test involves a reading booklet containing a number of pieces of literature and non-fiction. There is a separate question booklet, in which children write their answers to questions. There are several formats of question throughout the paper. The time allowed for the reading test will be 45 minutes plus 15 minutes of reading time. The range of text types included in the reading test over the last five years have been narrative texts, information texts, opinion, letters, poetry, interviews and instructions. The test in any one year will focus on several different types of text. This test is externally marked and the marks and papers returned to the school. It is possible to appeal and have the test re-marked.

Most teachers prepare children quite explicitly for these tests. Preparation for the tests should not be limited to a small number of text types, but should focus on the skills involved in understanding and responding across the range of texts. The marking scheme indicates the main skills assessed for each question in the reading test and is essential reading for you if you are going to teach at Key Stage 2. Age-standardised scores are available for the reading test and although teachers do not have to use them they give a measure of how children have done relative to other children of the same age.

THE LEVELS 3-5 WRITING TEST

In the writing test children are given a choice from a range of four starting points, including narrative and non-narrative. The time allowed for the writing test is 45 minutes plus 15 minutes of planning time and children use the *Writing test instructions and planning sheet* provided with the English writing test to prepare for their writing. Schools must not substitute their own planning sheet or writing frame when administering the writing test. The marking of this writing test is quite different from the marking of the Key Stage 1 writing test. Each starting point has its own marking scheme and these focus on a range of composition criteria. Spelling and handwriting are not part of this test. This test is externally marked and the marks and papers returned to the school. It is possible to appeal and have the test re-marked.

THE LEVELS 3-5 SPELLING AND HANDWRITING TEST

All children undertake separate spelling and handwriting tests and are given scores for each. The spelling test takes about 10 minutes to complete and the handwriting test takes 5 minutes. The marks from the spelling and handwriting test are aggregated with the writing test marks and contribute to the overall writing level awarded. They will also be aggregated with the reading and writing test marks and contribute to the overall subject award at levels 3-5. Age-standardised scores are available for the spelling test so that children's marks can be compared with other children of the same age. This test is externally marked and the marks and papers returned to the school.

It is possible to appeal and have the test re-marked.

THE EXTENSION TEST (LEVEL 6)
Children assessed as working at level 6 take the extension test in addition to the levels 3-5 tests. Level 6 is awarded only if a child achieves sufficient marks in the levels 3-5 reading, writing, and spelling and handwriting tests to be awarded level 5 as well as sufficient marks in the extension test. The extension test includes some questions requiring extended answers. Children's responses will be marked in terms of testing reading and writing. The time allowed for the extension test is 60 minutes including reading time. This test is externally marked and the marks and papers returned to the school. It is possible to appeal and have the test re-marked.

AGE-STANDARDISED SCORES IN THE STATUTORY TESTS
Age-standardised scores are those which are adjusted to take account of the child's age. The level 2 and level 3 reading comprehension tests and the spelling test include tables to enable teachers to convert raw scores in these tests to age-standardised scores. The scores take account of the child's age when the tests were taken. These scores are available for schools to use on an optional basis. They will provide additional information which can be used where teachers wish to report to parents about the performance of individual children, for passing information to subsequent schools, and by headteachers and governors as additional management information.

Teacher assessment

Teacher assessment is an essential part of the National Curriculum assessment and reporting arrangements. At Key Stage 2, teachers assign levels for reading, writing, speaking and listening and do in-service training to check that they are levelling at the same standards. At both Key Stages speaking and listening is only assessed through teacher assessment. At Key Stage 2 grades for all four modes of language are submitted. The results from teacher assessment are reported alongside the test results. Both have equal status and provide complementary information about children's attainment. The tests provide a standard 'snapshot' of attainment at the end of the Key Stage, while teacher assessment, carried out as part of teaching and learning in the classroom, covers the full range and scope of the programmes of study, and takes account of evidence of achievement in a range of contexts, including that gained through discussion and observation. For children working at levels 1 and 2 in Key Stage 2, teacher assessment provides the sole means of statutory assessment.

Teachers are required to summarise their teacher assessments at the end of the Key Stage for each eligible child, in the form of:

- a level for *each attainment target* in English, mathematics and science;
- an *overall subject level* in each of these subjects, which must be calculated by aggregating the teacher assessment attainment target levels.

The level descriptions in the National Curriculum are the basis for judging children's levels of attainment at the end of the Key Stage. Level descriptions indicate the type and range of performance that children working at a particular level should characteristically demonstrate. Teachers should use their knowledge of a child's work to judge which level description best fits that child's performance across a range of contexts. The aim is for a rounded judgement which:

- **is based on knowledge of how the child performs over time across a range of contexts;**
- **takes into account strengths and weaknesses of the child's performance;**
- **is checked against adjacent level descriptions to ensure that the level awarded is the closest match to the child's performance in each attainment target.**

Two weeks before the end of the summer term, end of Key Stage teacher assessment levels must be finalised and must be submitted to the national data collection agency.

Schools are required to keep records on every child, including information on academic achievements, other skills and abilities and progress made in school. They must update these records at least once a year.

Reporting to parents

Headteachers are responsible for ensuring that they send a written report to parents on their child's achievements at least once during the school year. *The Education (Pupil Information) (England) Regulations 2000* prescribe the minimum content of children's reports. Schools may issue more than one report, provided that the minimum information is sent to parents by the end of the summer term.

Where information, such as the results of National Curriculum assessments, is not available before the end of the summer term, headteachers must ensure that it is sent to parents as soon as practicable, and, in any case, no later than 30 September. The requirements for school reports at Key Stage 2 are detailed below.

For all children in Years 3, 4, 5 and 6:

- **brief comments on the child's progress in each subject and activity studied as part of the school curriculum – these should highlight strengths and development needs;**
- **the child's general progress;**
- **arrangements for parents to discuss the report with a teacher at the school;**
- **total number of sessions (half days) attended and the total number of sessions missed through authorised absence since the child's last report or since the child entered the school, whichever is later, and the total number of sessions missed through unauthorised absence.**

Additional information for children at the end of Key Stage 2:

- **the child's National Curriculum assessment levels. The list below sets out what must be reported:**

- a statement that the levels have been arrived at by statutory assessment;
- a statement where any attainment target has been disapplied for a child under sections 364 or 365 of the Education Act 1996;
- a brief commentary setting out what the results show about the child's progress in the subject individually and in relation to other children in the same year, drawing attention to any particular strengths and weaknesses;
- the percentage of children at the school at each level of attainment at the end of Key Stage 2;
- the national percentage of children at each level of attainment at the end of Key Stage 2.

Writing reports to parents

Parents are almost universally interested in their children's school performance and yet do not always feel they have detailed information. This means that reports are very important. Reports should be written for parents in a clear and straightforward way. Most parents want to know:

- **how their child is performing in relation to their potential and past achievements, to the rest of the class, and national standards;**
- **their child's strengths and any particular achievements;**
- **areas for development and improvement;**
- **how they can help;**
- **whether their child is happy, settled and behaving well.**

Reports should be personal to the child and there is evidence that some parents dislike statement banks or computer-generated reports when this makes them impersonal. The best computer-generated programs avoid this by offering a wide range of comments. If you do not use a computer-generated comment bank you should use attainment targets and the NLS to support your choice of vocabulary. The report should be well written and legible, with correct grammar, punctuation and spelling, but avoiding educational jargon. Comments should be as succinct as possible and use wording which is precise and appropriate.

A useful school report should concentrate on what the child has or has not learned, rather than what has been taught (many schools will already have informed their parents at the beginning of each term what will be taught during that term). A report should indicate what standards the child has achieved and whether any comparison is being made with his or her progress in other subjects, with previous performance, with other children in the class or against national standards. If a system of grading is used, either for attainment or effort, parents need a key or notes which will help them to understand the system, how different aspects, for example effort and attainment, relate to each other and, in the case of attainment, how it relates to national standards.

Reports can be an important way of helping children make progress and become aware of new targets. Children can be motivated by highlighting their strengths and recognising and valuing achievements in different areas of school life, but areas for development should be clearly identified and suggestions made about how these can be improved. It is important not to obscure low achievement or underachievement by the use of faint praise or by avoiding any mention of the problem. Reports should give an accurate picture of current attainment. They can then be used to involve the child in setting clear, achievable and time-related targets for his or her learning. Even the most able and conscientious child can be given suggestions about how to make further progress.

Parent meetings

Schools will usually have termly parents' meetings and for some this will be the only opportunity to discuss their child with the teacher. Remember that some parents will feel daunted by meeting teachers and you will need to put them at their ease. The meeting should provide an opportunity for them to ask questions and learn about their child's performance and attitude. Parents want teachers to be honest about their child's performance; most would rather have the full picture, even if this is uncomfortable.

During meetings with parents, teachers should have available their records of the child's work or scheme of work. These can be used to illustrate standards of work and other points made in discussions. Many parents appreciate specific advice about how to help their child improve, even where their child is already doing well.

Many schools maintain contact about children's progress in English through home-school books or homework books. These can include targets for children and advice for parents about how to help. The parents' meeting is a good time to remind parents about these forms of communications or to discuss misunderstandings.

Practical task

As part of your course you should make sure you write some English reports and discuss them with your school mentor. We suggest you write at least three:

- *a report for a child who is struggling with reading or writing;*
- *a report for a very articulate child;*
- *a report for a child you judge as 'average' for the class.*

Remember to include all aspects of English performance with an emphasis on achievements and targets.

Practical task

Below is an example of an end-of-year report for one Year 2 girl. You might want to read this as if you were the parent of this girl and comment on the level and preciseness of the information it offers.

Tarsem Kaur Daphu

English

Tarsem reads many types of books independently but shows a strong preference for fiction texts. She can give reasons why she likes her favourite authors and why she enjoys them. Tarsem knows how to find answers to questions using information books but sometimes finds the task onerous. In her writing, she chooses words and expressions carefully to create interesting, effective stories. She is less enthusiastic about report writing but is able to select salient points and structure reports well. In general, her spelling is sound, although she is not always accurate when she attempts irregular and unfamiliar words. Tarsem's contributions to class discussions show that she listens carefully. She takes a positive but understated part in group discussion and she is good at helping quieter children take part in joint activities. She is working above national expectations for her age.

Assessing English :

a summary of key points

- **Planning and assessment are the key to effective English teaching.**
- **There are a number of purposes for assessment so it is unlikely that one simple approach will meet them all.**
- **There are three basic approaches to assessment: analysing products, observing processes and questioning.**
- **Miscue analysis or running records can be very effective ways of assessing children's reading performance.**
- **You need to be fully aware of the statutory aspects of assessment and reporting to parents.**

Further Reading

QCA (1998) *Supporting the Target Setting Process: Guidance for Effective Target Setting for Pupils with Special Educational Needs.* London: DfEE/QCA.

alliteration A phrase in which adjacent or fairly closely connected words begin with the same phoneme.

analogy The perception of similarity between two things; relating something known to something new; in spelling, using known spellings to spell unknown words: *night-knight-right-sight-light-fright;* in reading, using knowledge of words to attempt previously unseen words.

analytical methods Approaches to teaching reading in which texts or sections of texts are introduced first, followed by an analysis of their constituent parts such as letters, phonemes and words.

audience The people addressed by a text. The term refers to listeners, readers of books, film/TV audiences and users of information technology.

big book An enlarged text book suitable for use with a group of children during shared reading.

blends The process of combining phonemes into larger elements such as clusters, syllables and words. Also refers to a combination of two or more phonemes, particularly at the beginning and end of words, e.g. *st, str, nt, pl, nd.*

brainstorming The process of collecting ideas on a particular topic without evaluating or classifying them. This can be useful as a precursor to writing as it allows plenty of ideas to be generated. A subsequent stage is to sort and evaluate the ideas amassed.

composition The process of developing ideas during writing.

comprehension Understanding of a phenomenon. It is usually qualified, e.g. reading comprehension, listening comprehension.

demonstrations These occur when teachers show children how to perform tasks such as reading or writing.

dialect A regional dialect refers to the features of grammar and vocabulary that convey information about a person's geographical origin.

digraph A written representation of a sound using two letters. Consonant digraphs represent consonant sounds (/ch/ in cheese). Vowel digraphs represent vowel sounds but may use letters we usually call consonants (/ae/ in pain, station, say). Sometimes the two letters making up the digraph are separated (/a/ and /e/ in late) and this is known as a split digraph. When one sound is represented by three letters (/tch/ in match) this is known as a trigraph.

editing Modifying written work, either own or another's, in preparation for publication. This process takes place after *drafting* (composition) and *revising* (major restructuring) and before *proof-reading* (a final check for typographical, spelling errors, etc). It involves checking of facts, minor improvements to style at sentence level, and checking for accuracy and agreement.

extended writing A piece of writing for which a longer period of time is required than that available within the literacy hour format.

formative assessment Assessment of pupils' ongoing work.

genre A collection of linguistic practices and narrative conventions that govern the way particular texts are written for particular purposes.

graphic cues Clues used to recognise words in reading which derive from letter shapes and patterns.

graphophonic cue A combination of reading cues using letter shapes and sound–symbol correspondences.

guided reading A classroom activity in which pupils are taught in groups according to reading ability. The teacher works with each group on a text carefully selected to offer an appropriate level of challenge to the group.

guided writing A classroom activity in which pupils are grouped by writing ability. The teacher works with each group on a task carefully selected to offer an appropriate level of challenge to the group.

hot seating A drama activity in which a child is asked to play a particular role and answer questions in that role.

literacy A communication skill. The term *literacy* is most often applied to written communication but it can also be applied to other forms, as in *media literacy, computer literacy.*

metalanguage The language we use when talking about language itself. It includes words like *sentence, noun, paragraph, preposition.*

metalinguistic awareness An awareness of how language works. This is an umbrella term which includes such forms of awareness as phonological awareness, syntactic awareness, etc.

miscue A misreading of a word or group of words. It is possible, using miscue analysis, to determine some of the reasons behind this misreading, which often rest in the reader's use of the cueing systems of reading.

mnemonics A device to aid memory, for instance to learn particular spelling patterns or spellings: *I Go Home Tonight; There is a rat in separate.*

onset The consonant(s) which precede the nucleus of a syllable: s-un. Some syllables have no onset: eel.

oracy The skill of using speaking and listening to communicate. It parallels literacy.

phoneme The smallest contrastive unit of sound in a word.

phonemic segmentation Ability to split words into their constituent phonemes.

phonic cues Clues used to recognise words in reading which derive from knowledge of sound-symbol correspondences.

phonics A method of teaching children to read by teaching them to recognise and use sound-symbol correspondences.

phonological awareness Awareness of units of sound in speech.

prefixes A prefix is a morpheme which can be added to the beginning of a word to change its meaning, for example: *in*edible, *dis*appear, *super*market.

reading comprehension Understanding of a read text.

register The term used by linguists to indicate the different ways in which people speak to different audiences for different purposes.

revision Making structural changes to a piece of writing one is composing. It should be distinguished from *editing.*

rime The part of a syllable which contains the syllable nucleus (usually a vowel) and final consonants, if any – b-in.

semantic cues Clues used to recognise words in reading which derive from knowledge of the meaning of the text.

sentence level A level of knowledge about the way text works which includes knowledge of grammar and punctuation.

sentence level work Teaching activities focused on sentence level knowledge.

shared reading In shared reading the teacher, as an expert reader, models the reading process by reading the text to the learners. The text chosen may be at a level that would be too difficult for the readers to read independently. The teacher demonstrates the use of cues and strategies such as use of letter sounds, rereading, etc.

shared writing A classroom process where the teacher models the writing process for children: free from the physical difficulties of writing, children can observe, and subsequently be involved in, planning, composition, redrafting, editing and publishing through the medium of the teacher.

standard English Standard English is the variety of English used in public communication, particularly in writing. It is the form taught in schools and used by educated speakers. It is not limited to a particular region and can be spoken with any accent.

suffixes A suffix is a morpheme that is added to the end of a word to either change the tense or grammatical status of a word, e.g. from present to past (work*ed*) or from singular to plural (accident*s*), or to change the word class, e.g. from verb to noun (work*er*) or from noun to adjective (accident*al*).

summative assessment Assessment of pupils' work that occurs at the end of a fixed period, e.g. a year, or a unit of work.

syntactic cues Clues used to recognise words in reading which derive from knowledge of sentence grammar.

synthesising methods Approaches to teaching reading in which letters, phonemes and words are introduced first and then used to construct sentences or longer texts.

text level A level of knowledge about the way text works which includes knowledge of text structure and convention.

text-level work Teaching activities focused on text level knowledge.

transcription The process of transferring ideas to paper or screen in writing. It is distinguished from composition which is the process of developing the ideas.

word level A level of knowledge about the way text works which includes knowledge of word construction.

word-level work Teaching activities focused on word level knowledge.

writing frames Structured prompts to support writing. A writing frame often takes the form of opening phrases of paragraphs and may include suggested vocabulary. It often provides a template for a particular text type.

Adams, M. (1990) *Beginning to Read: Thinking and Learning about Print*. Cambridge, MA: MIT Press.

Barrs, M. and Thomas, A. (eds) (1991) *The Reading Book*. London: Centre for Language in Primary Education.

Bissex, G. (1980) *GNYS AT WRK: A Child Learns to Read and Write*. Cambridge, MA: Harvard University Press.

Bradley, L. and Bryant, P. (1985) *Children's Reading Problems*. Oxford: Blackwell.

Browne, A. (1999) *Teaching Writing at Key Stage I and Before*. London: Thomas Nelson.

Cairney, T. (1990) *Teaching Reading Comprehension*. Milton Keynes: Open University Press.

Cambourne, B. (1988) *The Whole Story*. Leamington Spa: Scholastic.

Chambers, A. (1993) *Tell Me: Children, Reading and Talk*. Gloucester: Thimble Press.

Clay, M. (1979) *The Early Detection of Reading Difficulties*. London: Heinemann.

Clipson-Boyles, S. (1998) *Drama in Primary English*. London: David Fulton.

Crystal, D. (1987) *The Cambridge Encyclopaedia of Language*. Cambridge: Cambridge University Press.

Crystal, D. (1995) *The Cambridge Encyclopaedia of the English Language*. Cambridge: Cambridge University Press.

Department for Education and Employment (1998) *The National Literacy Strategy: Framework for Teaching*. London: DfEE.

Department for Education and Employment (1998) *Teaching: High Status, High Standards (Requirements for Courses of Initial Teacher Training)*, Circular Number 4/98. London: DfEE.

Department for Education and Employment/Qualifications and Curriculum Authority (1999) *English: the National Curriculum for England*. London: HMSO.

Department for Education and Employment/Qualifications and Curriculum Authority (2000) *Curriculum Guidance for the Foundation Stage*. London: QCA.

Department for Education and Science (DES) (1978) *Primary Education in England*. London: HMSO.

Department for Education and Science (DES) (1991) *Education Observed: The Implementation of the Curricular Requirements of the ERA in 1989–90*. London: HMSO.

Dombey, H. and Moustafa, M. (1998) *Whole to Part Phonics*. London: CLPE.

Evans, J. (ed.) (2000) *The Writing Classroom*. London: David Fulton.

Gentry, R. (1982) 'An analysis of developmental spelling in GNYS AT WRK', *The Reading Teacher*, vol. 36 (2).

Goodman, K. S. (1976) 'Reading: a psychological guessing game', in H. Singer and R. B. Ruddell (eds), *Theoretical Models and Processes of Reading*. Newark, DE: International Reading Association.

Goodman, K., Goodman Y. and Burke C. (1978) 'Reading for life: the psycholinguistic base', in E. Hunter-Grundin and H. Grundin *Reading: Implementing the Bullock Report*. United Kingdom Reading Association.

Goodman, Y., Watson, D. and Burke, C. (1987) *Reading Miscue Inventory*. New York: Richard Owen.

Goodwin, P. (ed.) (1999) *The Literate Classroom*. London: David Fulton.

Goswami, U. and Bryant, P. (1990) *Phonological Skills and Learning to Read*. London: Lawrence Erlbaum.

Grainger, T. (1997) *Traditional Storytelling in the Primary Classroom*. Leamington Spa: Scholastic.

Graves, D. (1983) *Writing: Teachers and Children at Work*. Portsmouth, NH: Heinemann.

Halliday, M. A. K. (1978) *Language as a social semiotic: The social interpretation of language and meaning*. London: Edward Arnold.

Halliday, M. A. K. (1985) *An Introduction to Functional Grammar*. London: Edward Arnold.

Harste, J., Woodward, V. and Burke, C. (1984) *Language Stories and Literacy Lessons*. Portsmouth, NH: Heinemann.

Heathcote, D. and Bolton, G. (1995) *Drama for Learning: An Account of Dorothy Heathcote's 'Mantle of the Expert'*. Portsmouth NH: Heinemann.

Hodson, P. and Jones, D. (2001) *Teaching Children to Write*. London: David Fulton.

Kavanagh, J. and Mattingley, I. (eds) (1972) *Language by Ear and by Eye*. Cambridge, MA: MIT Press.

Ketch, A. (1991) 'The Delicious Alphabet', *English in Education*, vol. 25, (1).

Lewis, M. and Wray D. (1994) *Developing Children's Non-Fiction Writing*. Leamington Spa: Scholastic.

Lewis, M. and Wray, D. (1997) *Writing Frames*. Reading: University of Reading Reading and Language Information Centre.

Lewis, M. and Wray, D. (1998) *Writing across the Curriculum*. Reading: University of Reading Reading and Language Information Centre.

Littlefair, A. (1991) *Reading All Types of Writing*. Milton Keynes: Open University Press.

Lunzer, E. and Gardner, K. (1979) *The Effective Use of Reading*. Oxford: Heinemann.

Martin, J. (1989) *Factual Writing*. Oxford: Oxford University Press.

Meek, M. (1982) *Learning to Read*. London: Bodley Head.

Minns, H. (1997) *Read It to Me Now! Learning at Home and at School*. Buckingham: Open University Press.

Peters, M. (1985) *Spelling: Caught or Taught*. London: Routledge.

Phinn, G. (2000) *Young Readers and their Books*. London: David Fulton.

Qualifications and Curriculum Authority (1998) *Supporting the Target Setting Process: Guidance for Effective Target Setting for Pupils with Special Educational Needs*. London: DfEE/QCA.

Qualifications and Curriculum Authority (1999) *Early Learning Goals*. London: QCA.

Sassoon, R. (1990) *Handwriting: The Way to Teach It*. Cheltenham: Stanley Thornes.

Southgate, V., Arnold, H. and Johnson, S. (1981) *Extending Beginning Reading*. Oxford: Heinemann.

Stanovich, K. E. (1984) 'The interactive-compensatory model of reading: a confluence of developmental, experimental and educational psychology', *Remedial and Special Education*. vol. 5, pp. 11–19.

Wells, G. (1987) *The Meaning Makers: Children Learning and Using Language to Learn*. London: Hodder & Stoughton.

Wray, D. (1981) *Extending Reading Skills*. Lancaster: University of Lancaster.

Wray, D. (1985) *Teaching Information Skills through Project Work*. Sevenoaks: Hodder & Stoughton.

Wray, D. (1993) 'What do children think about writing?', *Educational Review*, vol. 45 (1), pp. 67–7.

Wray, D. and Lewis, M. (1992) 'Primary children's use of information books', *Reading*. vol. 26 (3), pp. 19–24.

Wray, D. and Lewis, M. (1997) *Extending Literacy*. London: Routledge.

Wray, D. and Medwell, J. (2002) *Teaching Literacy Effectively*. London: RoutledgeFalmer.

Achieving QTS

Our *Achieving QTS* series now includes nearly 20 titles, encompassing *Audit and Test*, *Knowledge and Understanding*, *Teaching Theory and Practice*, and *Skills Tests* titles. As well as covering the core primary subject areas, the series addresses issues of teaching and learning across both primary and secondary phases. The Teacher Training Agency has identified books in this series as high quality resources for trainee teachers. You can find general information on each of these ranges on our website: www.learningmatters.co.uk

Primary English
Audit and Test (second edition)
Doreen Challen
£8 64 pages   ISBN: 1 903300 86 X

Primary Mathematics
Audit and Test (second edition)
Claire Mooney and Mike Fletcher
£8 52 pages   ISBN: 1 903300 87 8

Primary Science
Audit and Test (second edition)
John Sharp and Jenny Byrne
£8 80 pages   ISBN: 1 903300 88 6

Primary English
Knowledge and Understanding (second edition)
Jane Medwell, George Moore, David Wray, Vivienne Griffiths
£15   224 pages   ISBN: 1 903300 53 3

Primary English
Teaching Theory and Practice (second edition)
Jane Medwell, David Wray, Hilary Minns, Vivienne Griffiths, Elizabeth Coates
£15   192 pages   ISBN: 1 903300 54 1

Primary Mathematics
Knowledge and Understanding (second edition)
Claire Mooney, Lindsey Ferrie, Sue Fox, Alice Hansen, Reg Wrathmell
£15   176 pages   ISBN: 1 903300 55 X

Primary Mathematics
Teaching Theory and Practice (second edition)
Claire Mooney, Mary Briggs, Mike Fletcher, Judith McCullouch
£15   192 pages   ISBN: 1 903300 56 8

Primary Science
Knowledge and Understanding (second edition)
Rob Johnsey, Graham Peacock, John Sharp, Debbie Wright
£15   224 pages   ISBN: 1 903300 57 6

Primary Science
Teaching Theory and Practice (second edition)
John Sharp, Graham Peacock, Rob Johnsey, Shirley Simon, Robin Smith
£15   144 pages   ISBN: 1 903300 58 4

Primary ICT
Knowledge, Understanding and Practice (second edition)
Jane Sharp, John Potter, Jonathan Allen, Avril Loveless
£15   256 pages   ISBN: 1 903300 59 2

Professional Studies
Primary Phase (second edition)
Edited by Kate Jacques and Rob Hyland
£15   224 pages   ISBN: 1 903300 60 6

Teaching Foundation Stage
Edited by Iris Keating
£15   192 pages   ISBN: 1 903300 33 9

Teaching Humanities in Primary Schools
Pat Hoodless, Sue Bermingham, Elaine McReery, Paul Bowen
£15   192 pages   ISBN: 1 903300 36 3

Teaching Arts in Primary Schools
Stephanie Penny, Raywen Ford, Lawry Price, Susan Young
£15   192 pages   ISBN: 1 903300 35 5

Learning and Teaching in Secondary Schools
Edited by Viv Ellis
£15   192 pages   ISBN: 1 903300 38 X

Passing the Numeracy Skills Test (third edition)
Mark Patmore
£8   64 pages   ISBN: 1 903300 94 0

Passing the Literacy Skills Test
Jim Johnson
£6.99   80 pages   ISBN: 1 903300 12 6

Passing the ICT Skills Test
Clive Ferrigan
£6.99   80 pages   ISBN: 1 903300 13 4

Succeeding in the Induction Year (second edition)
Neil Simco
£13   144 pages   ISBN: 1 903300 93 2

To order, please contact:

Learning Matters Ltd
33 Southernhay East
Exeter EX1 1NX

Tel: 0845 230 9000
Fax: 01392 215 561
Email: orders@learningmatters.co.uk
www.learningmatters.co.uk